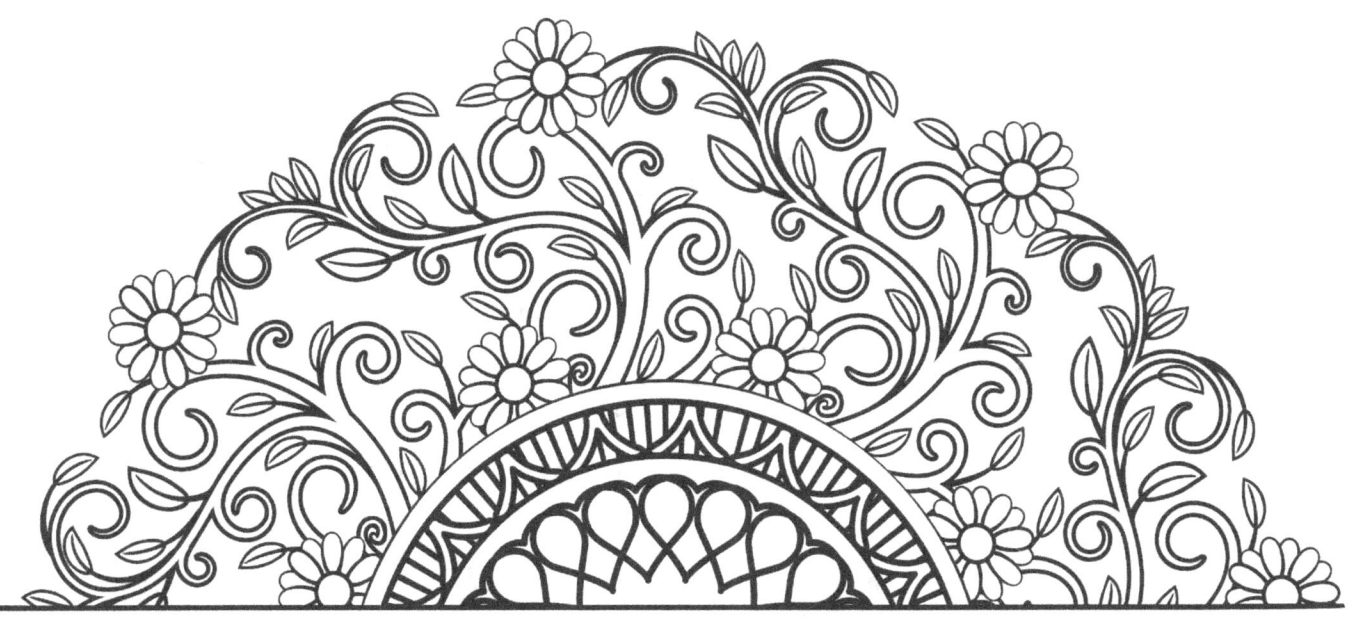

This Book Belongs To:

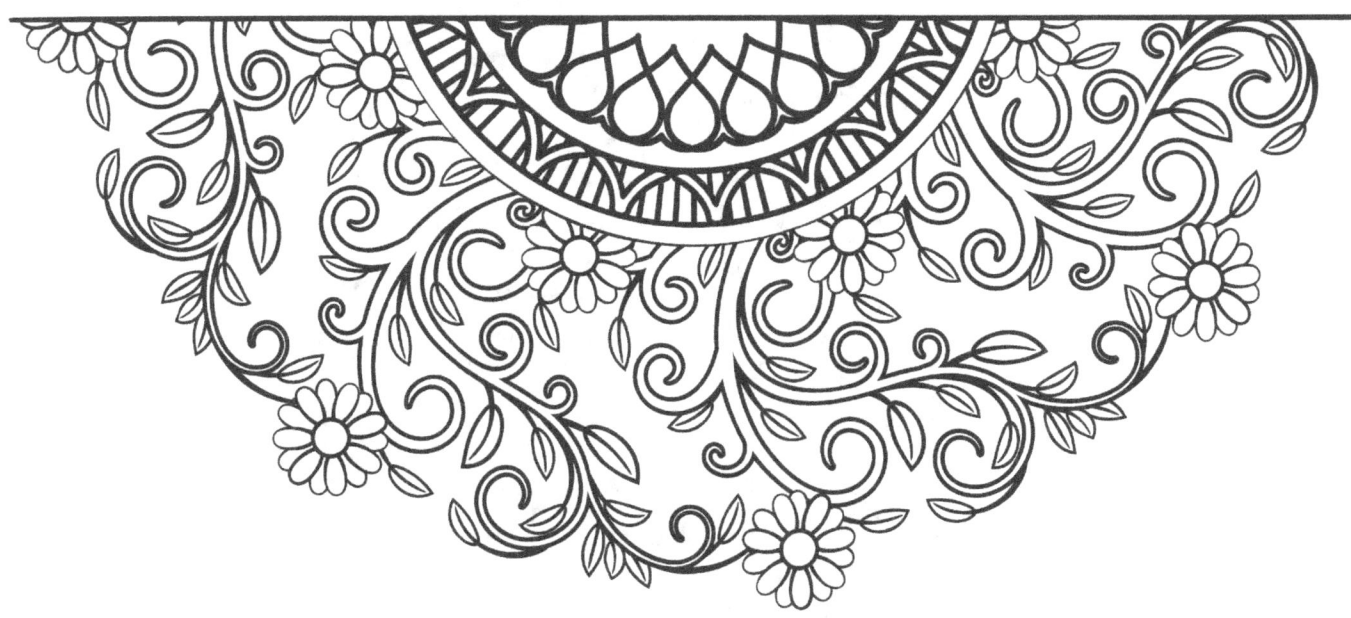

Zen Animals

Coloring Book

50 Calming Animal Designs

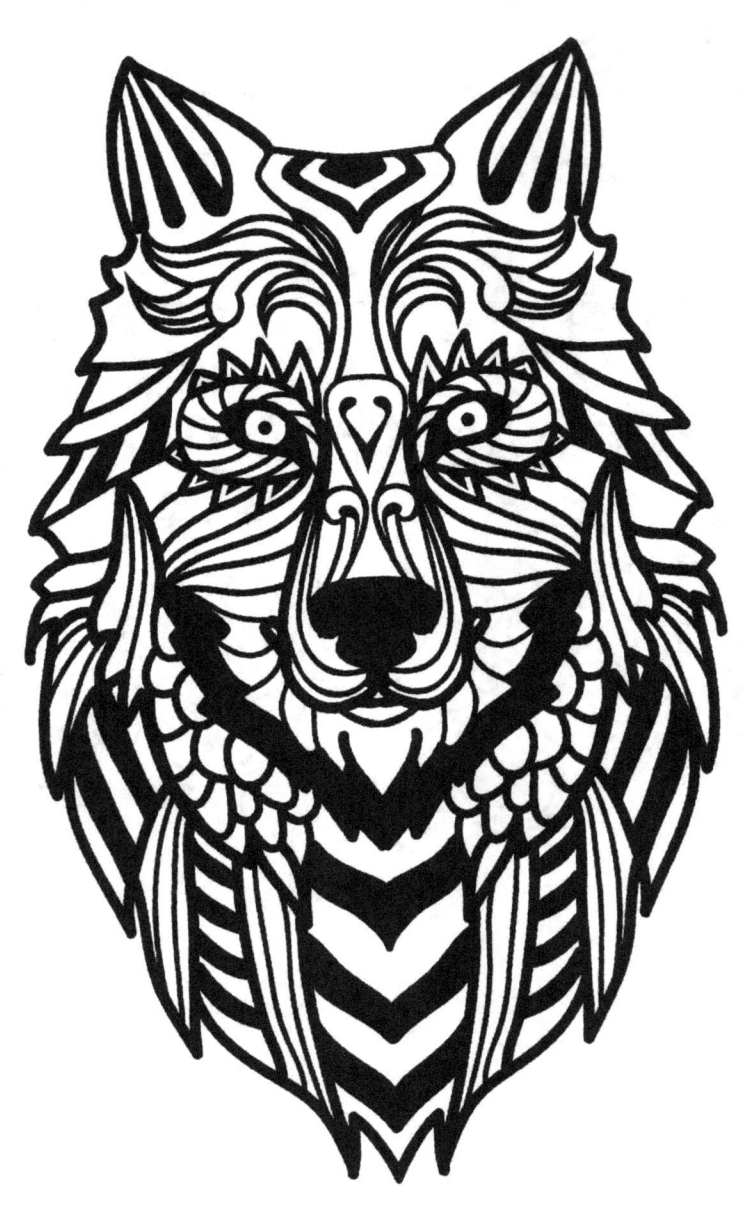

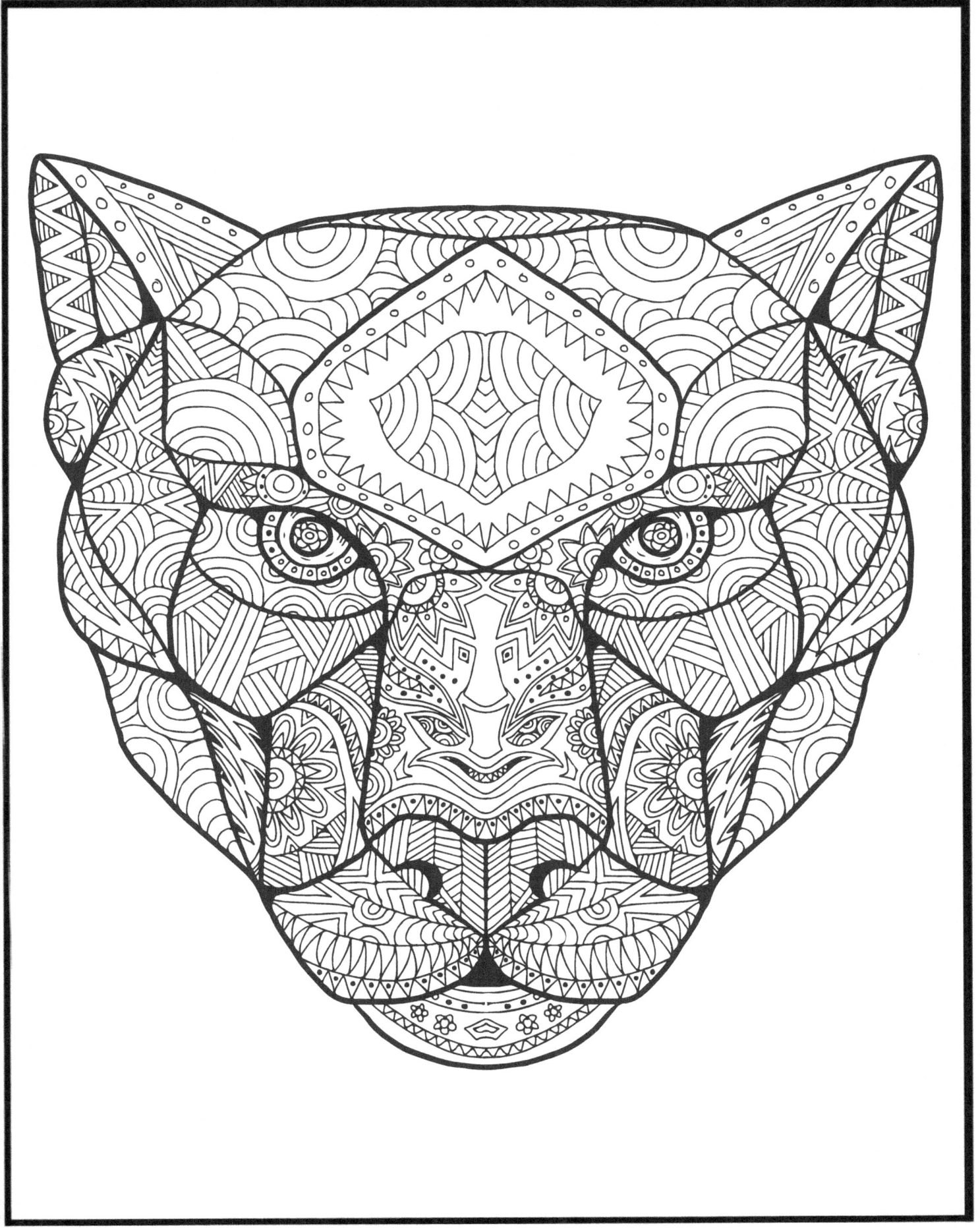

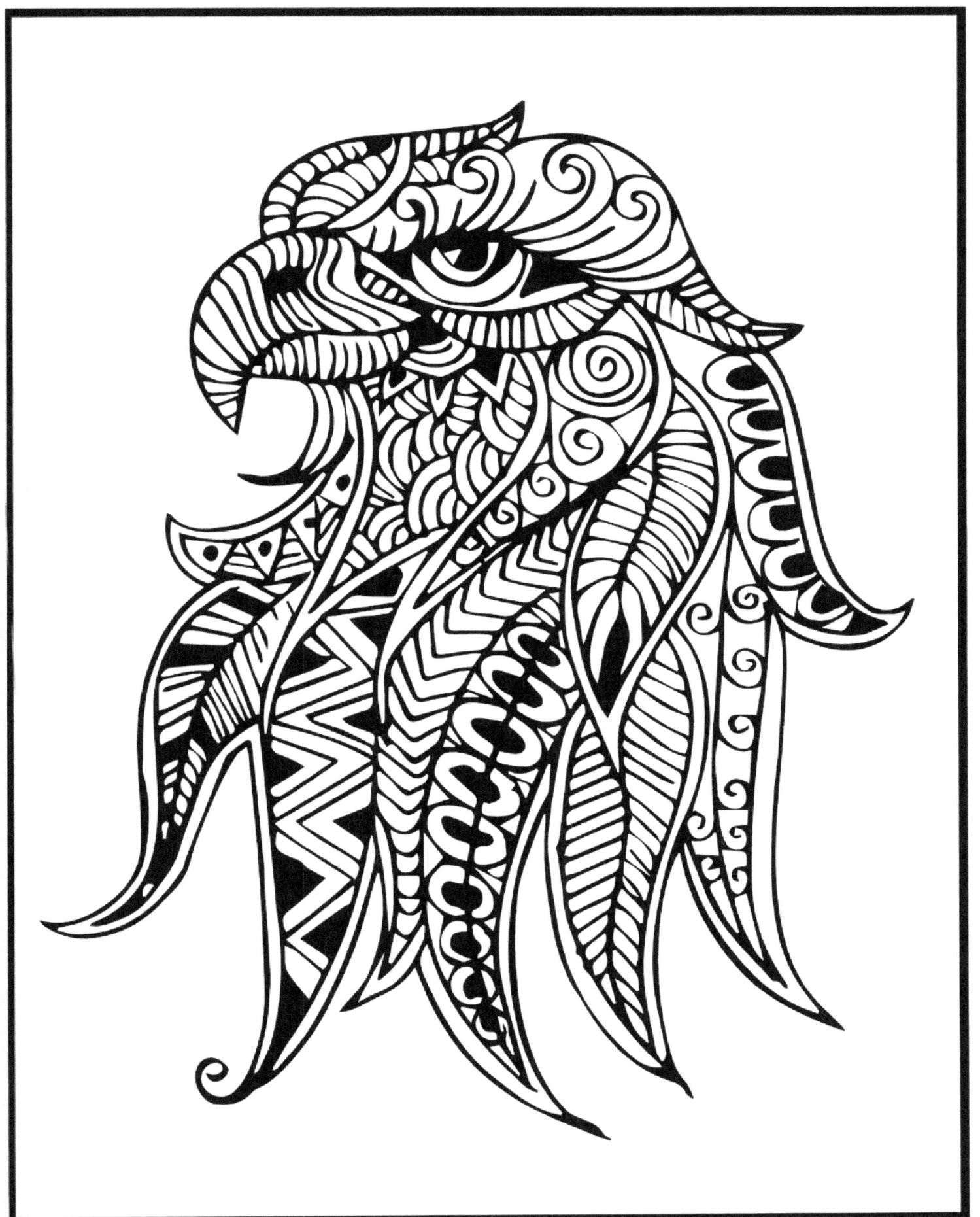

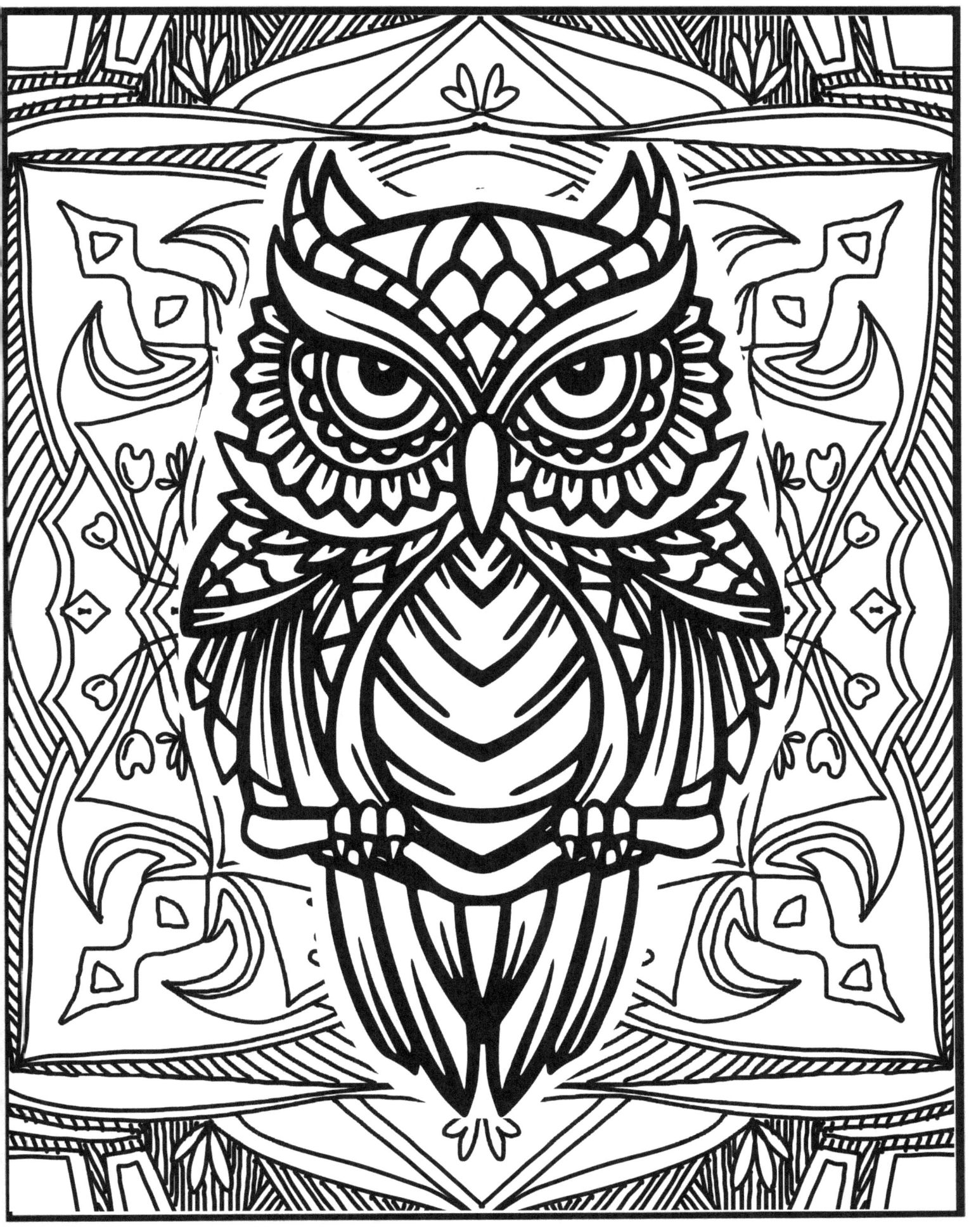

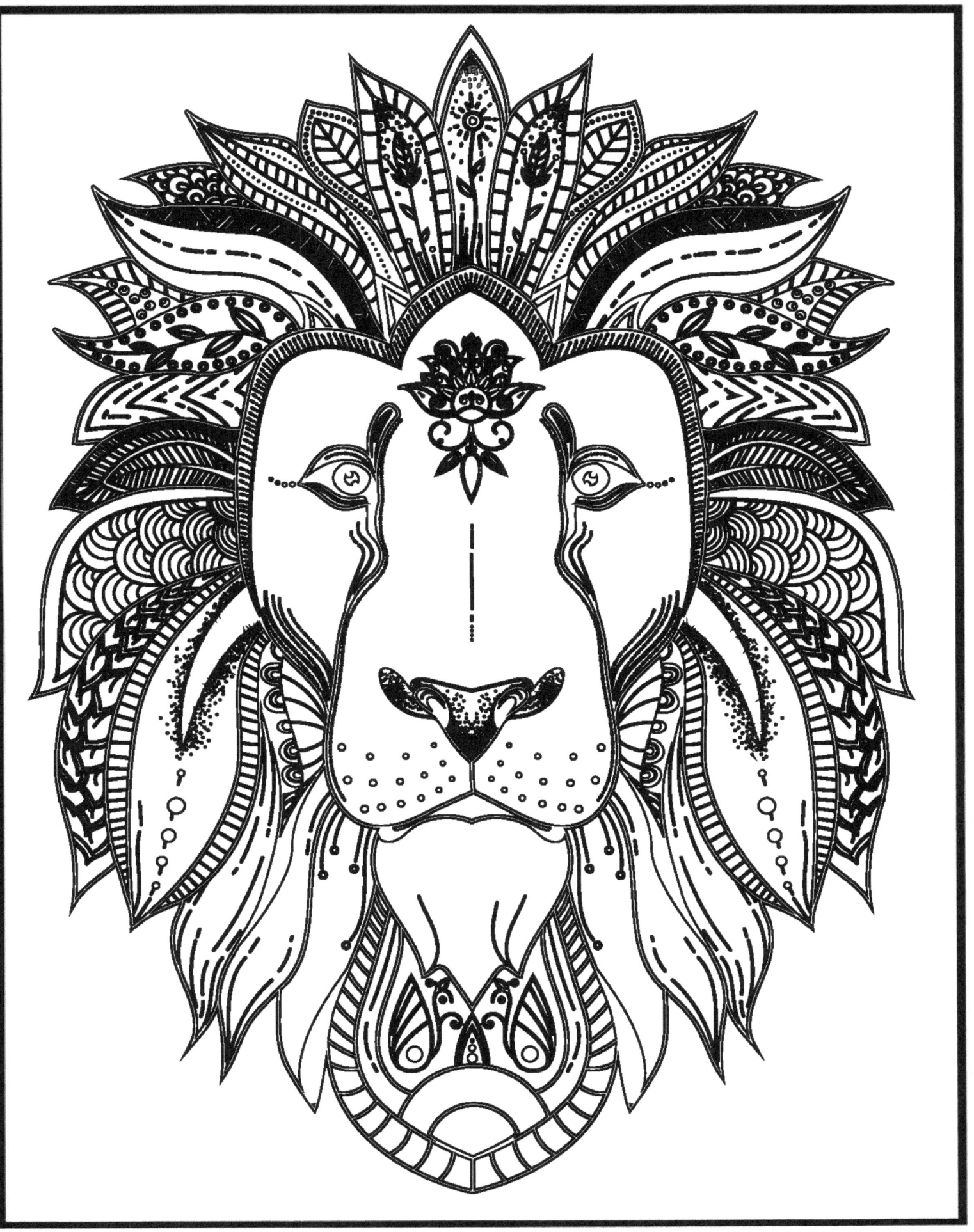

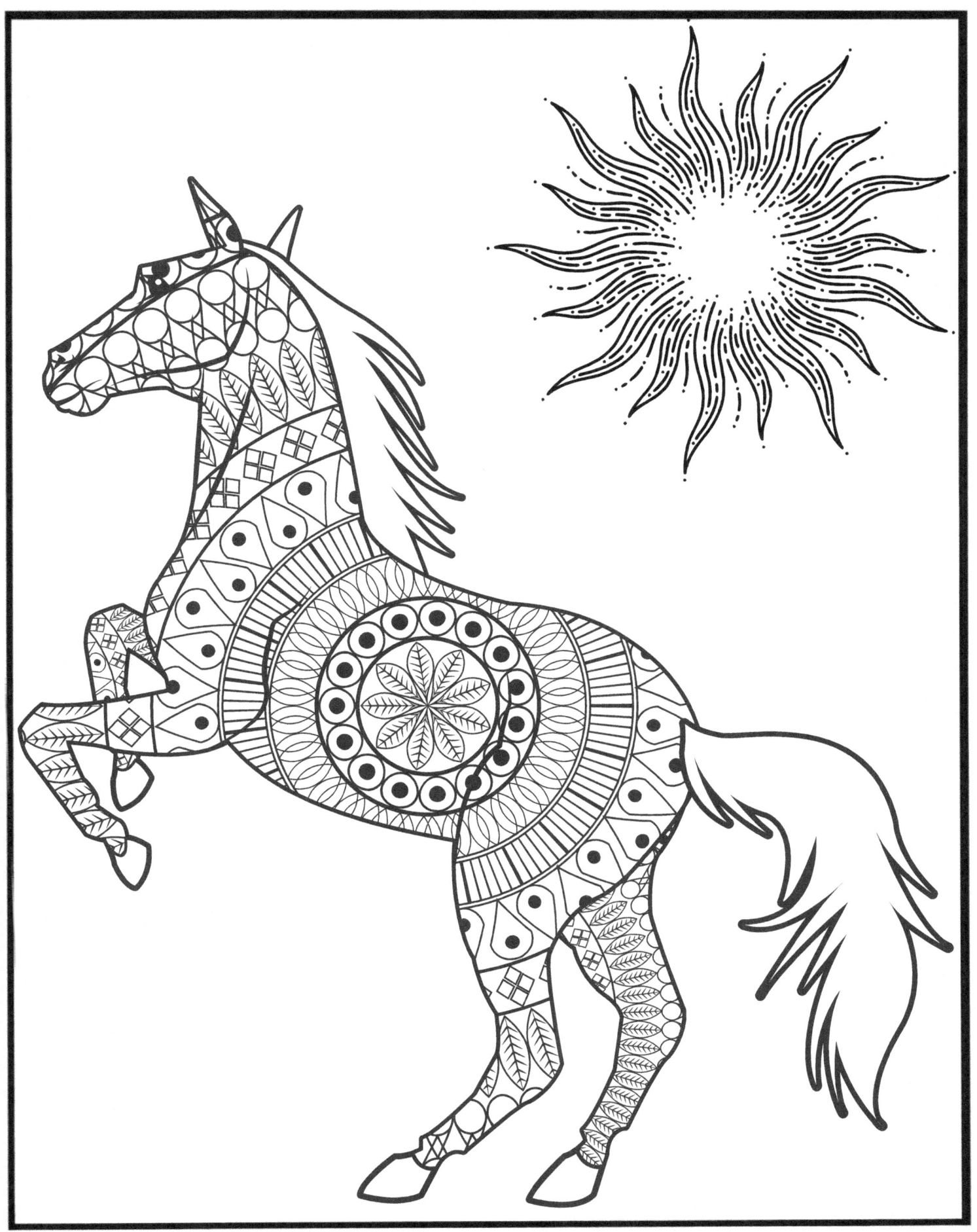

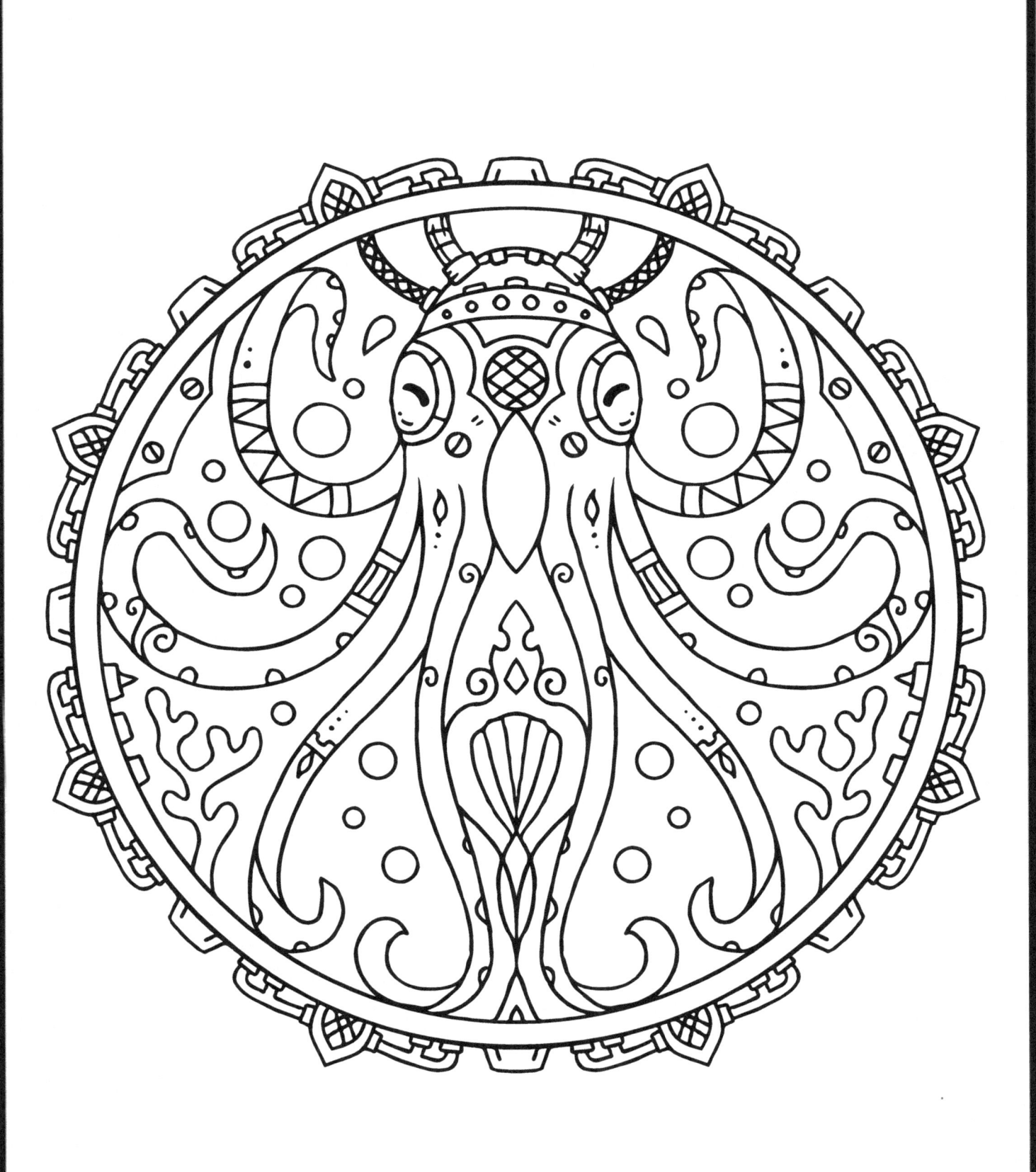

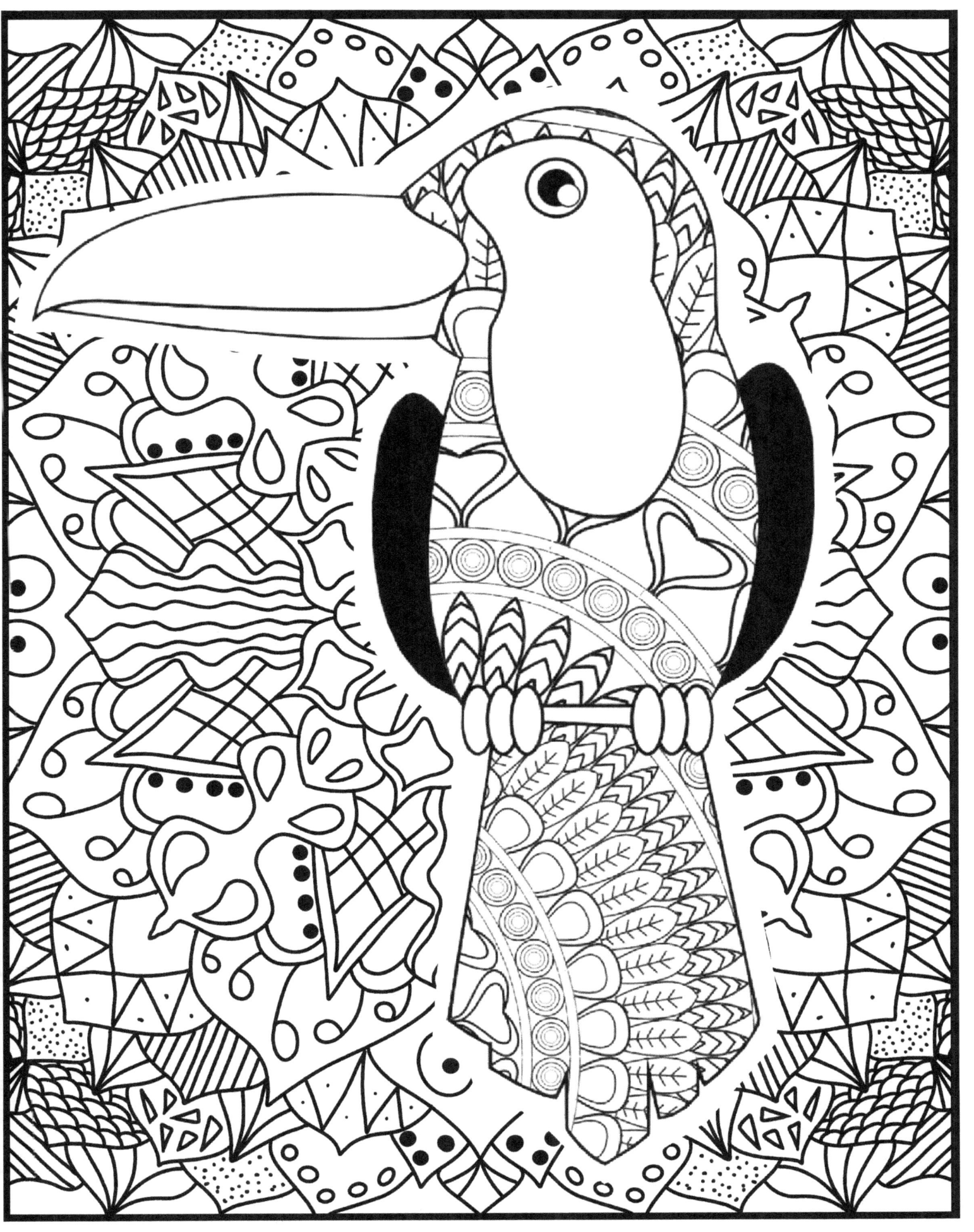

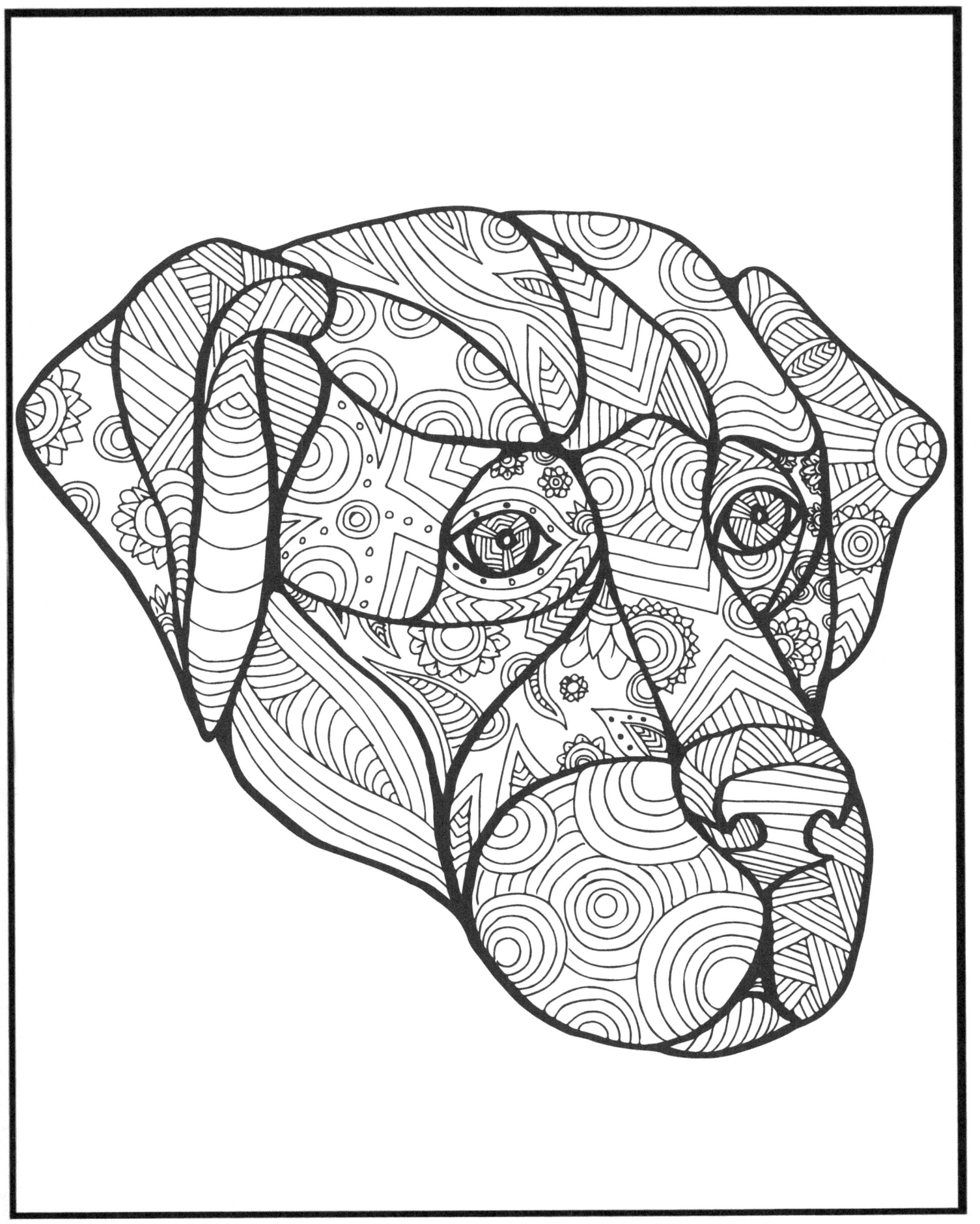

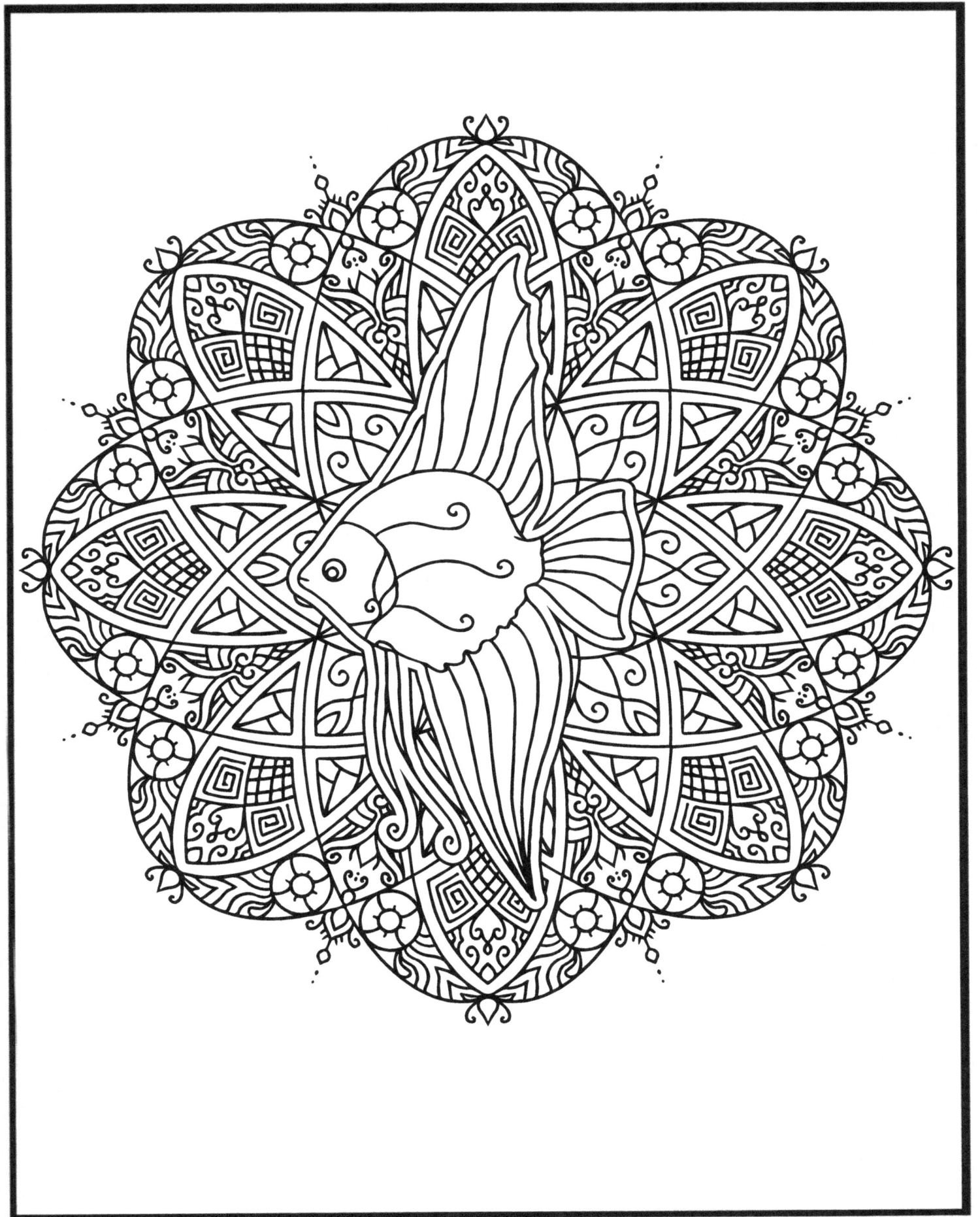

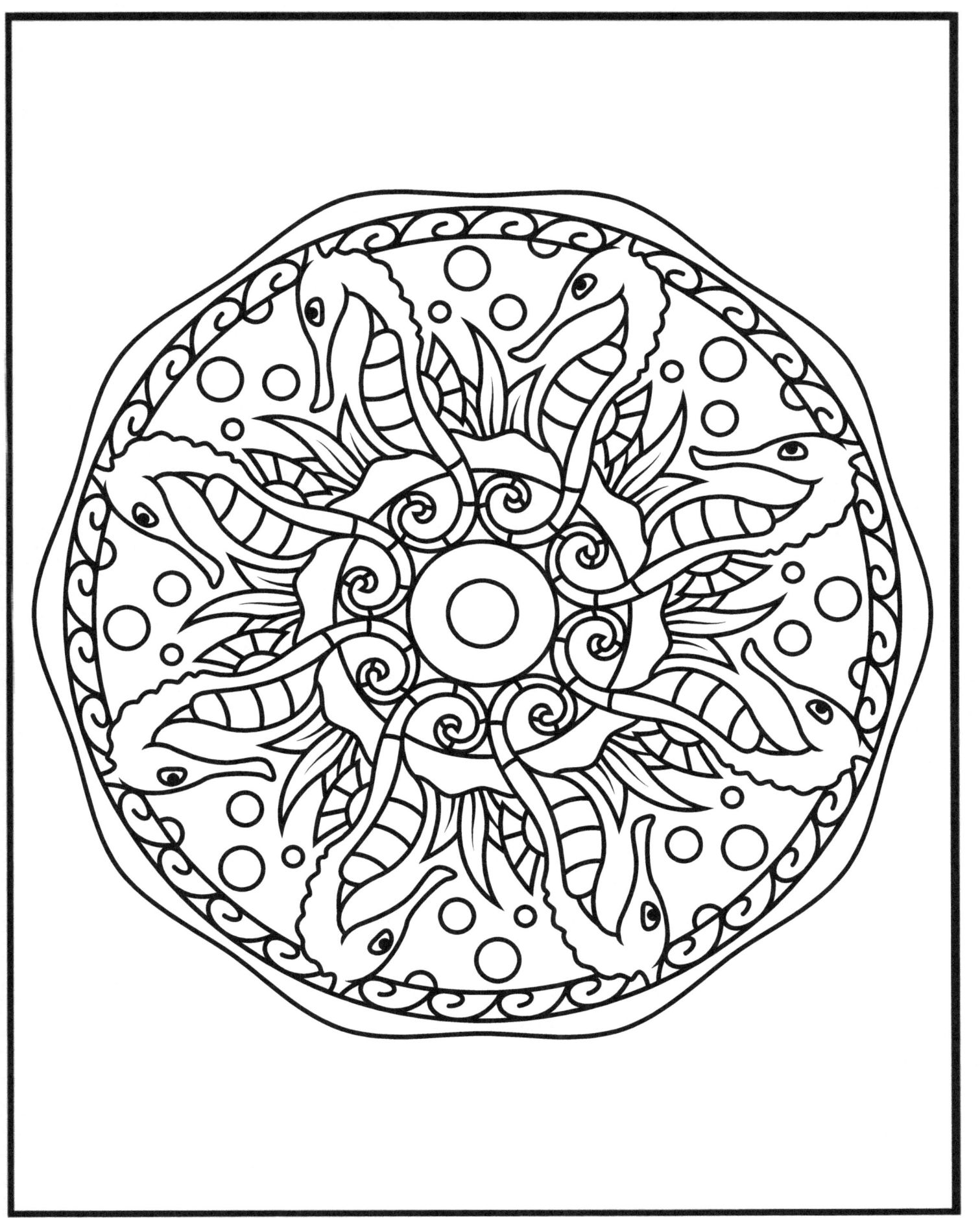

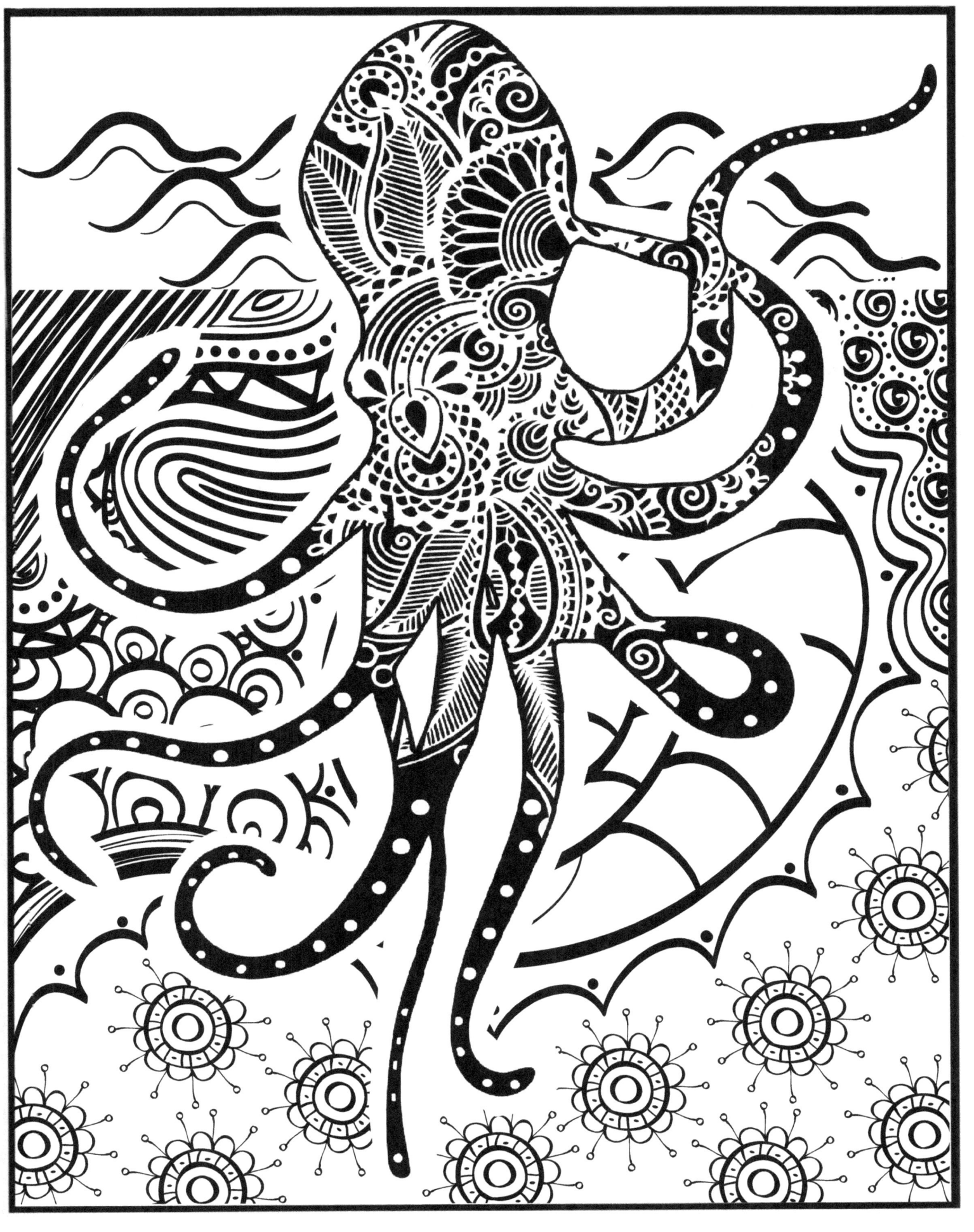

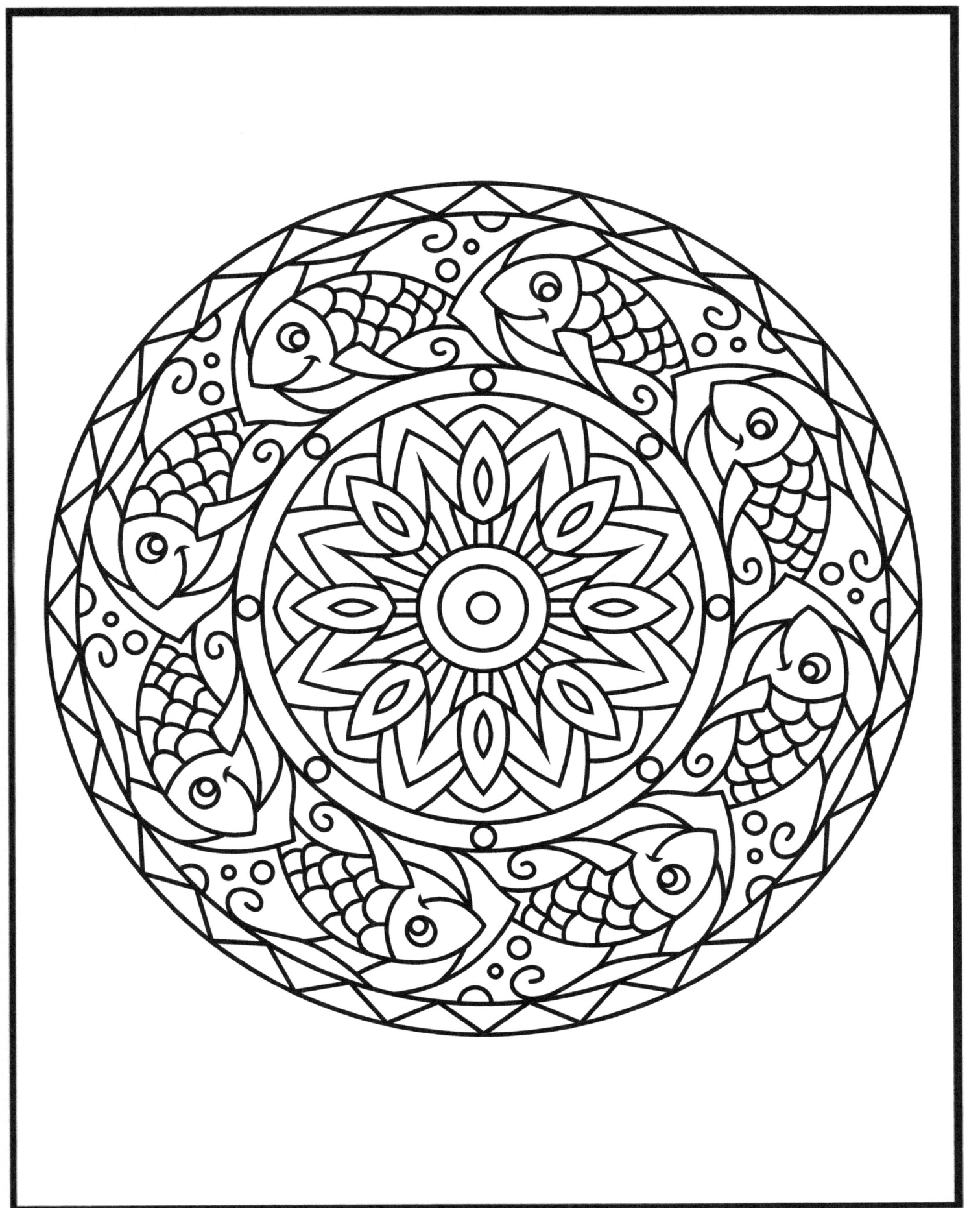

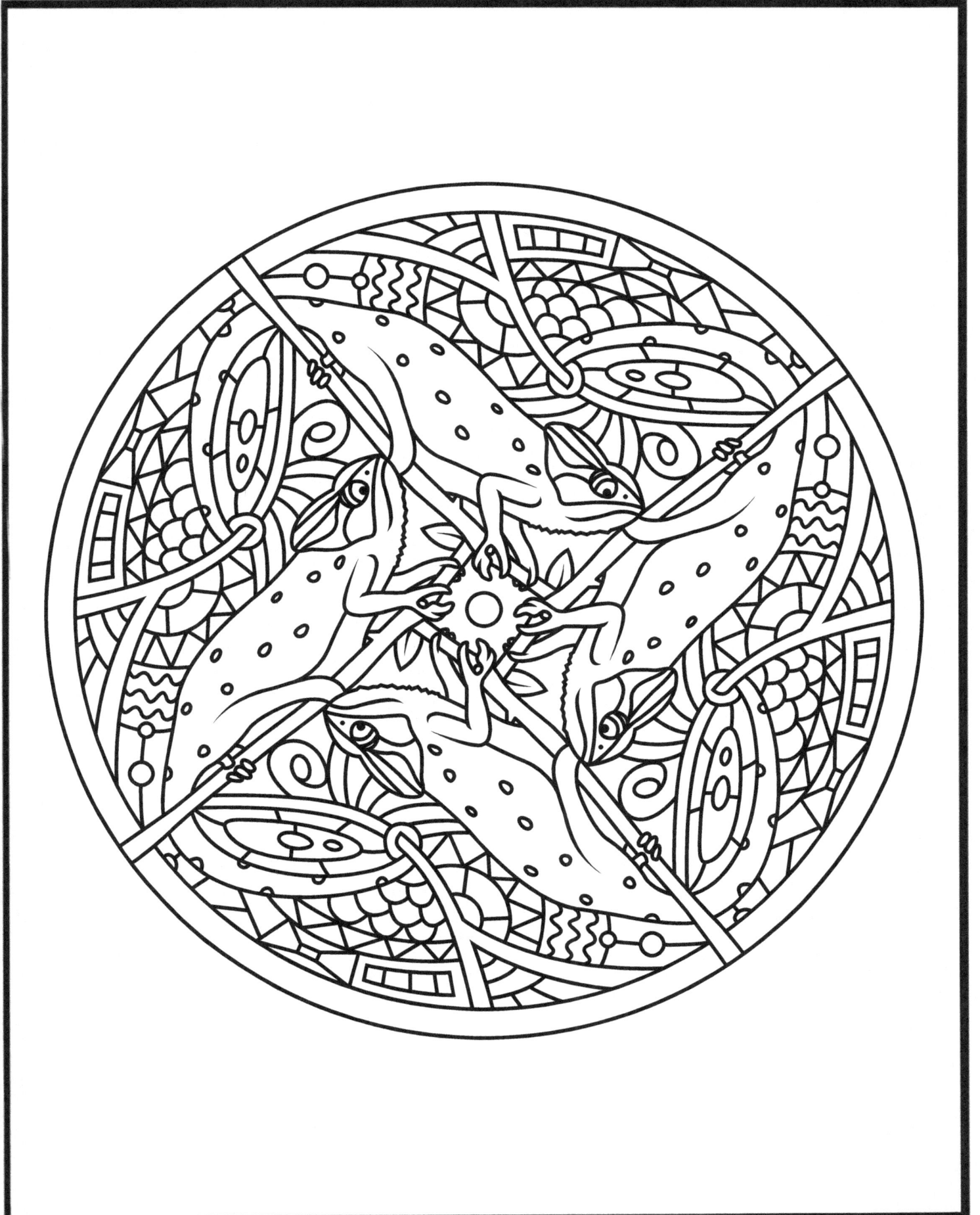

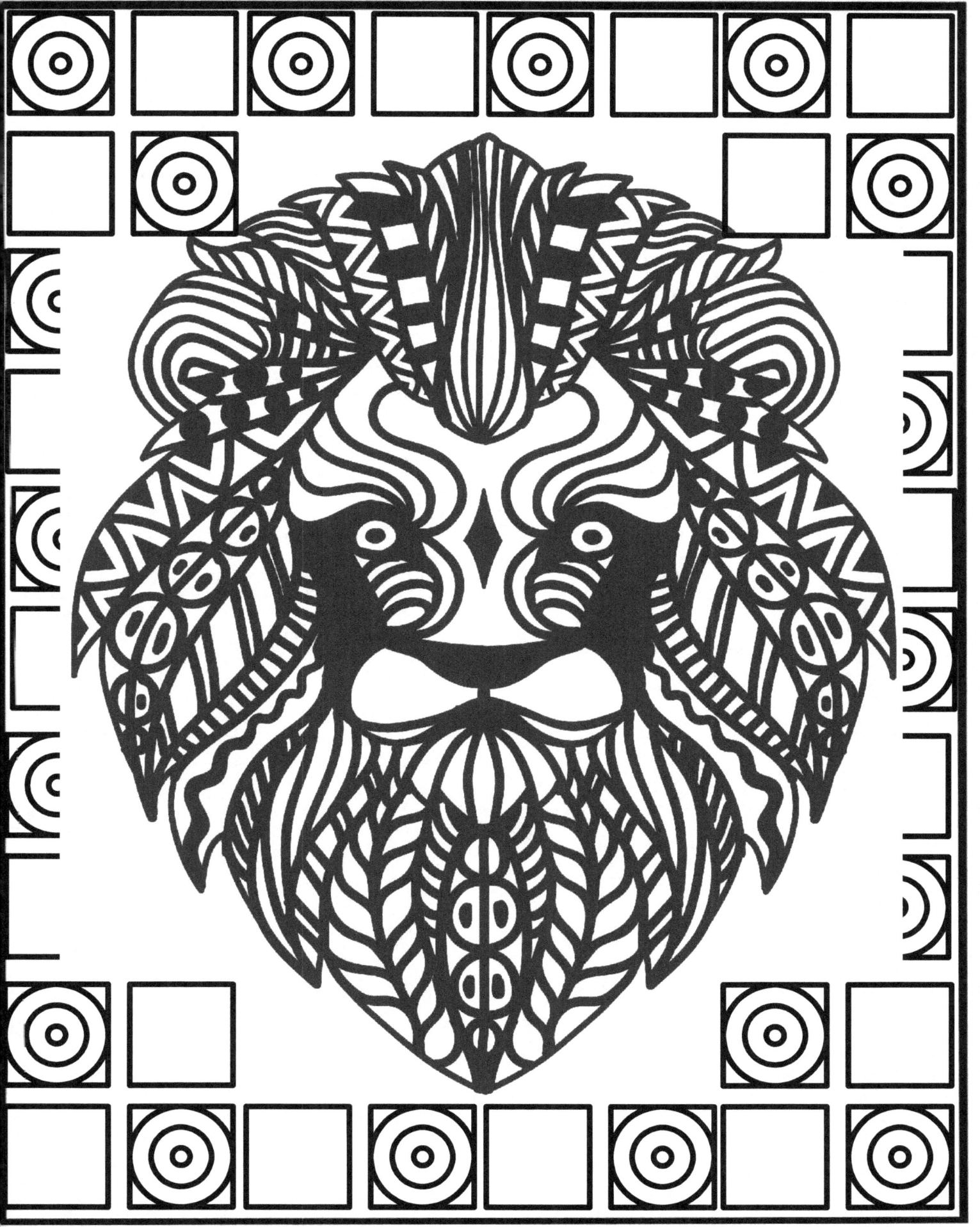

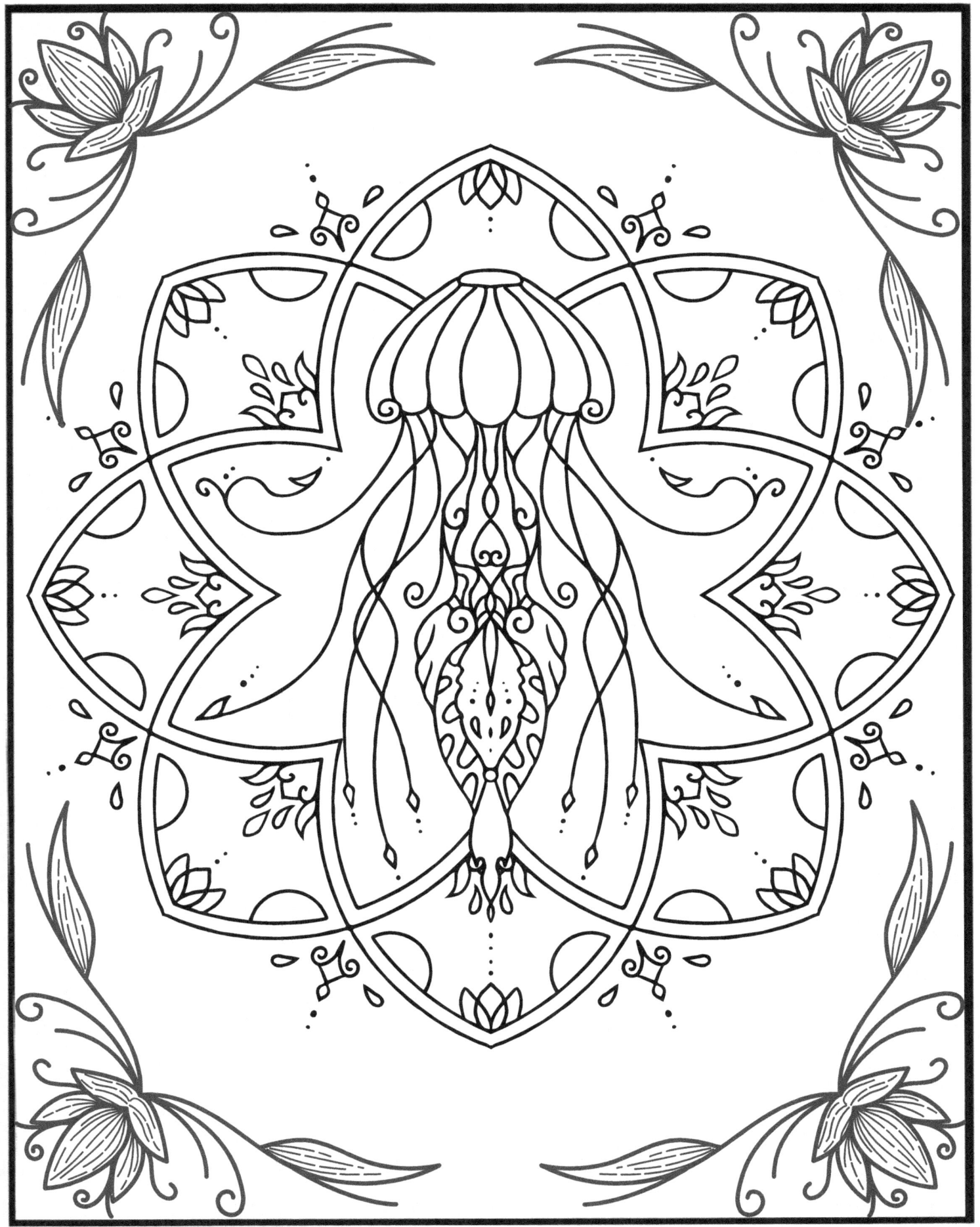

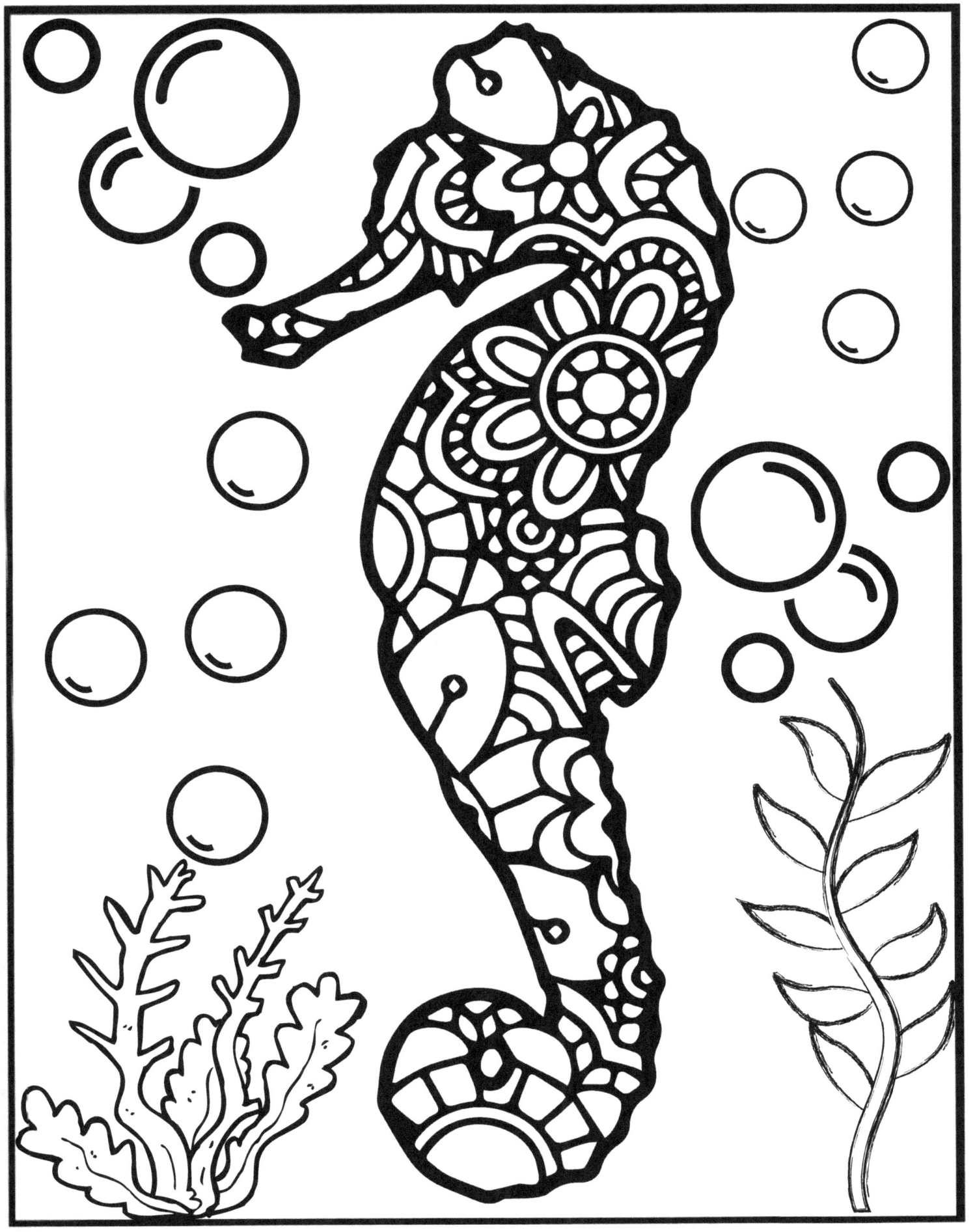

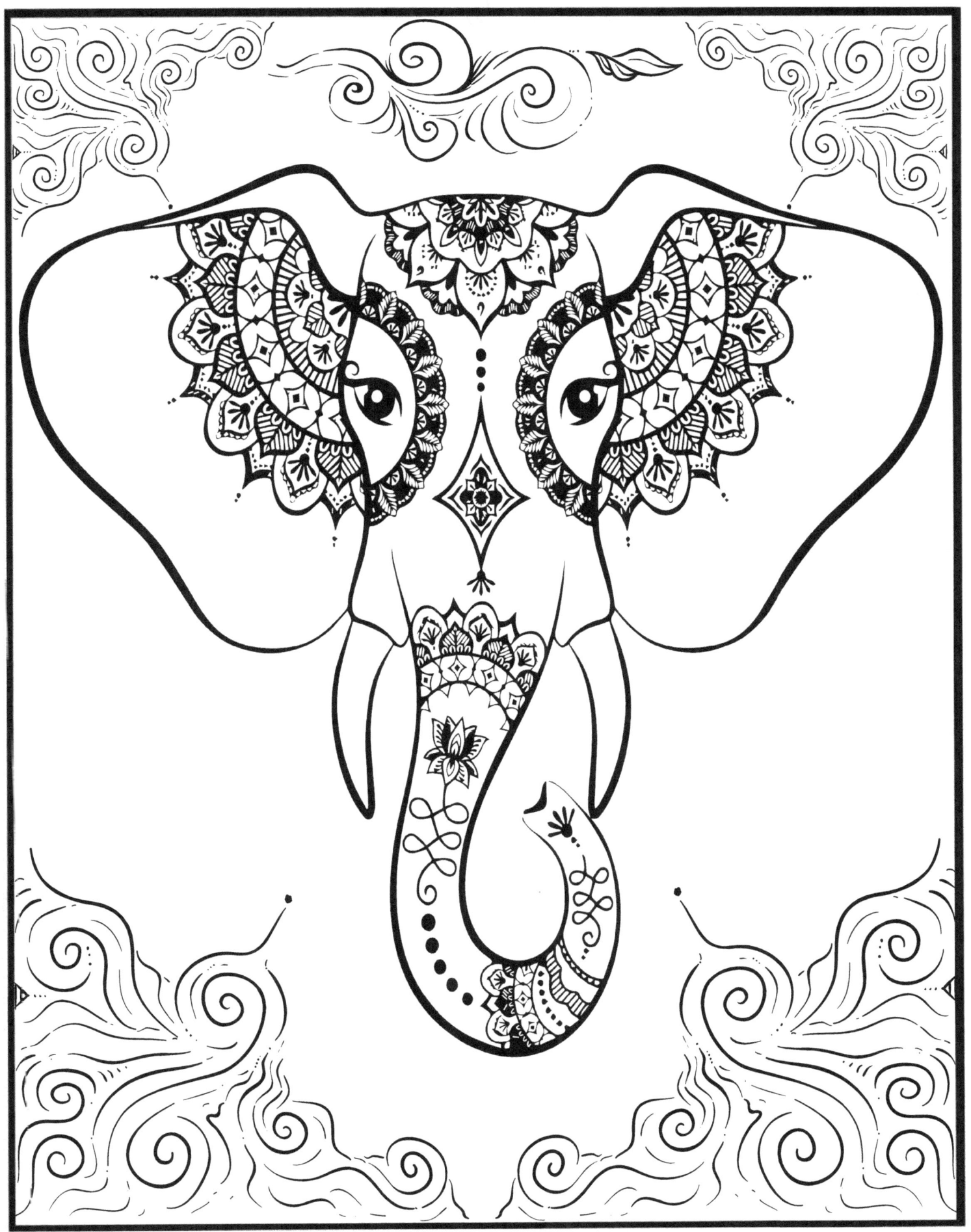

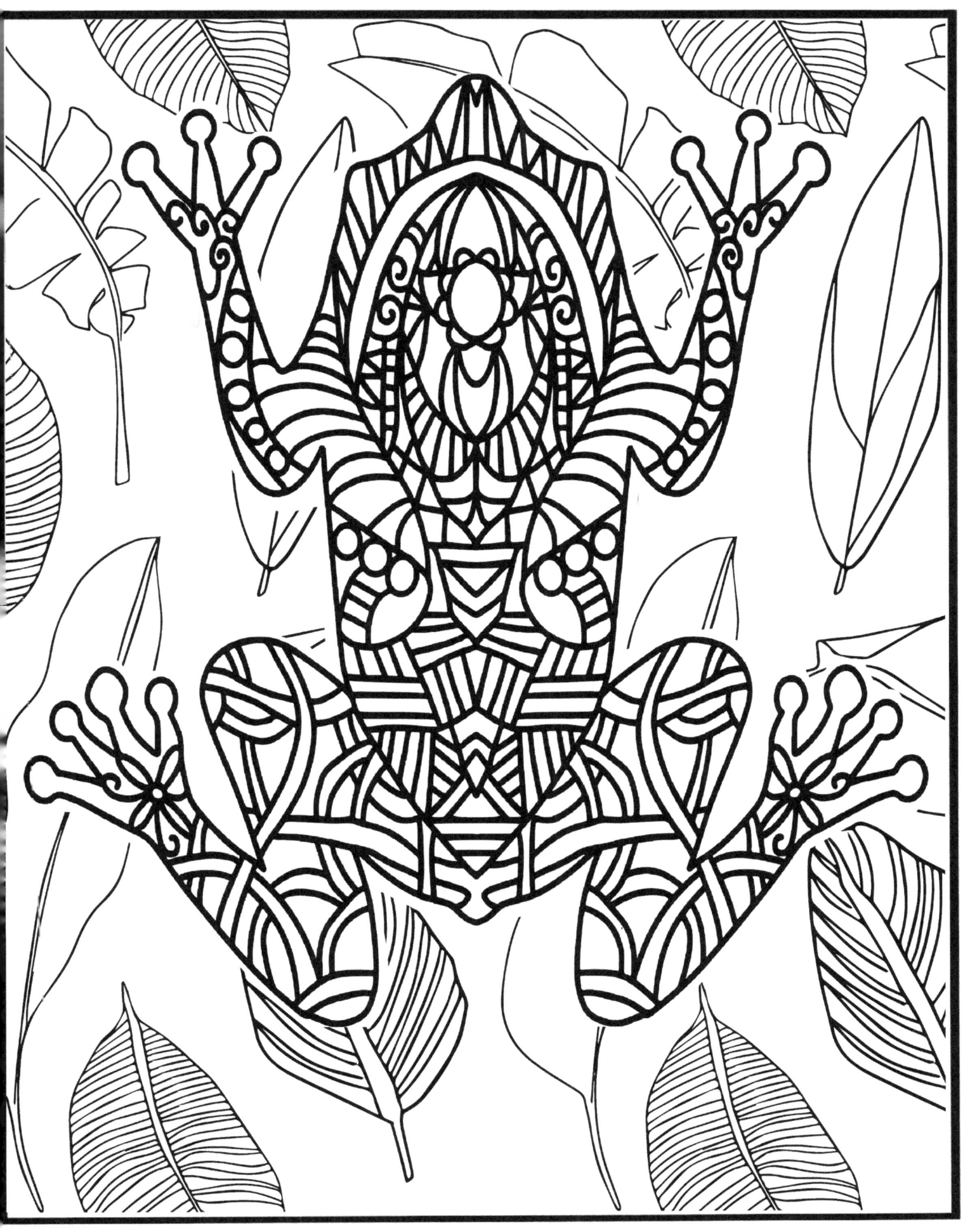

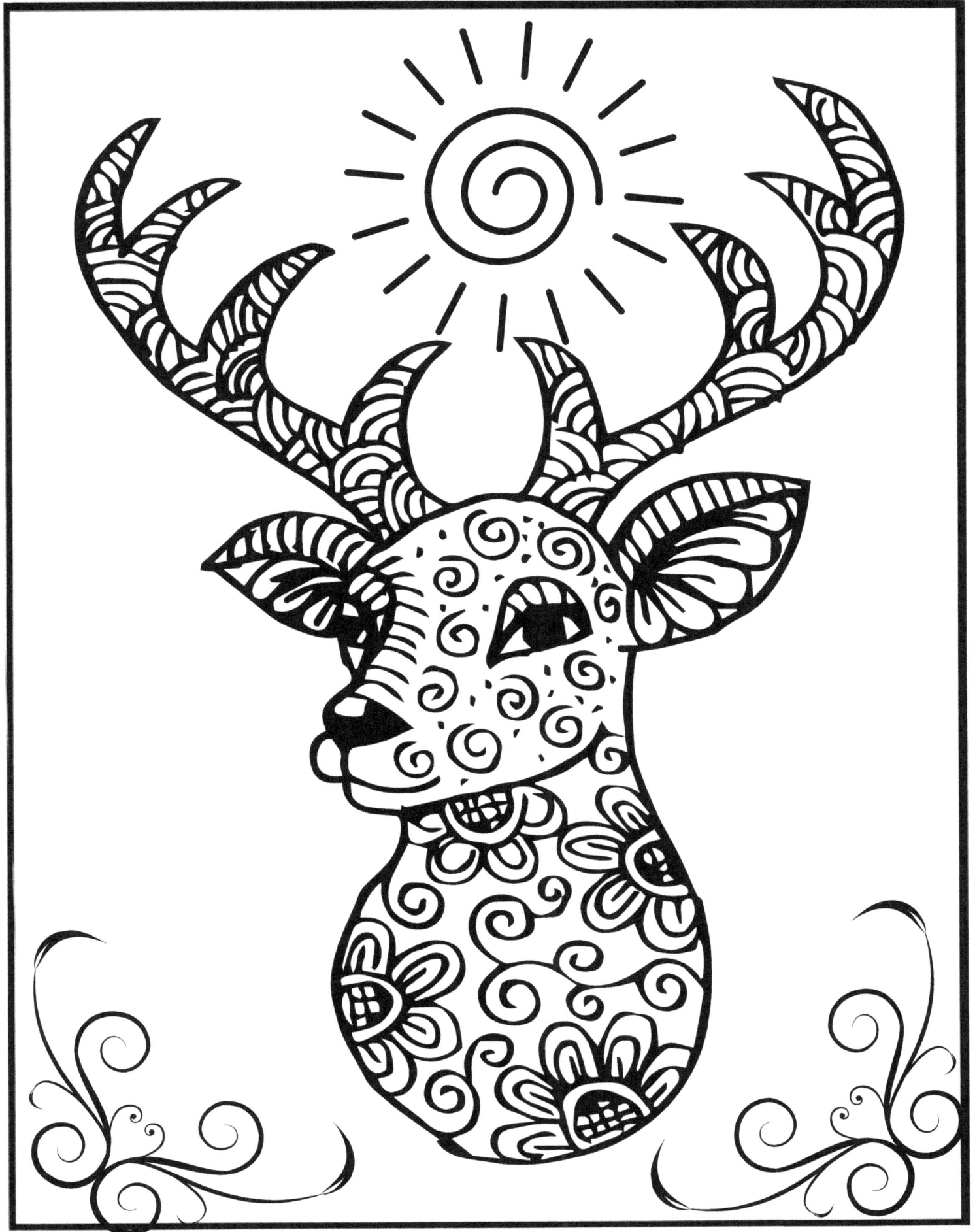

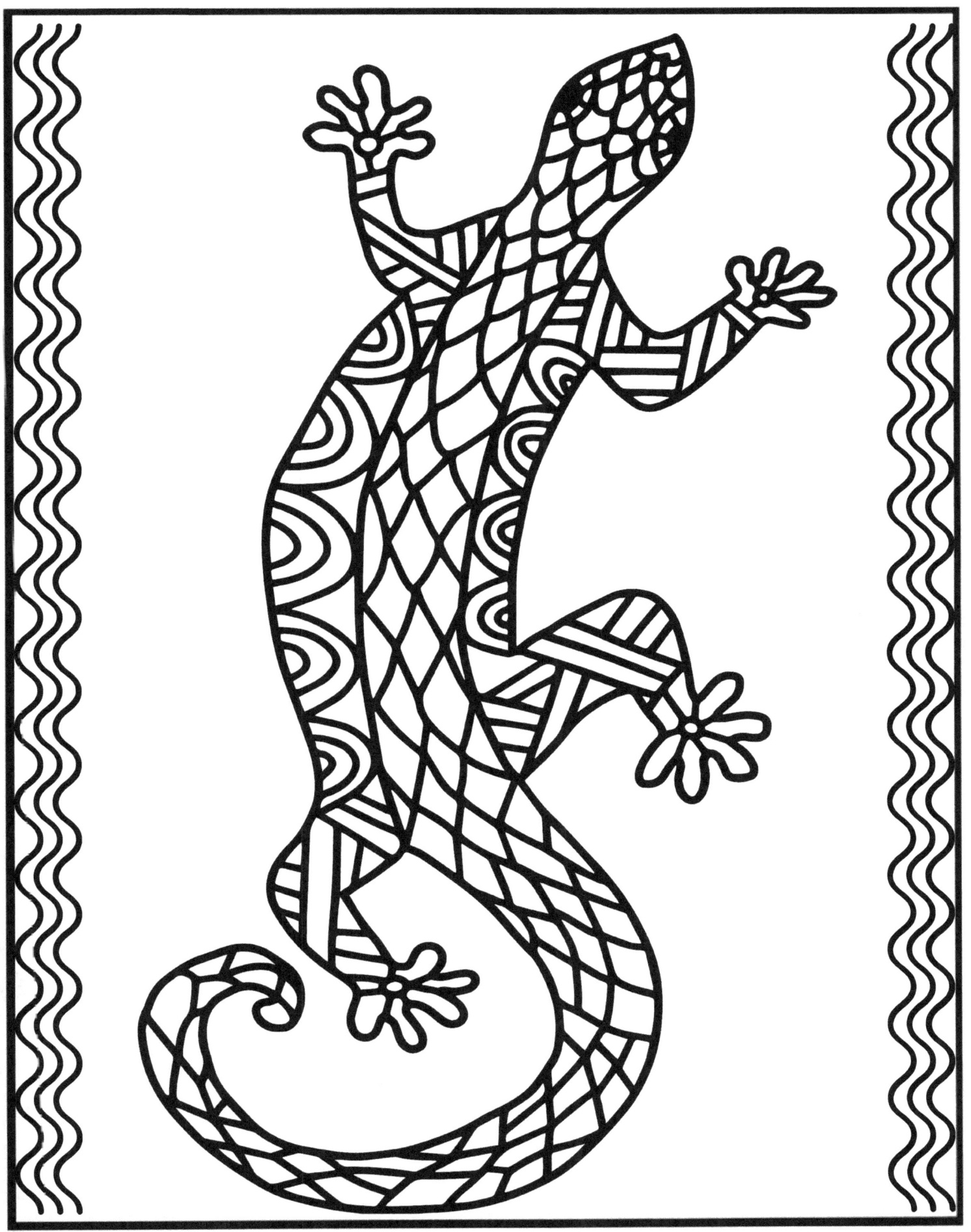

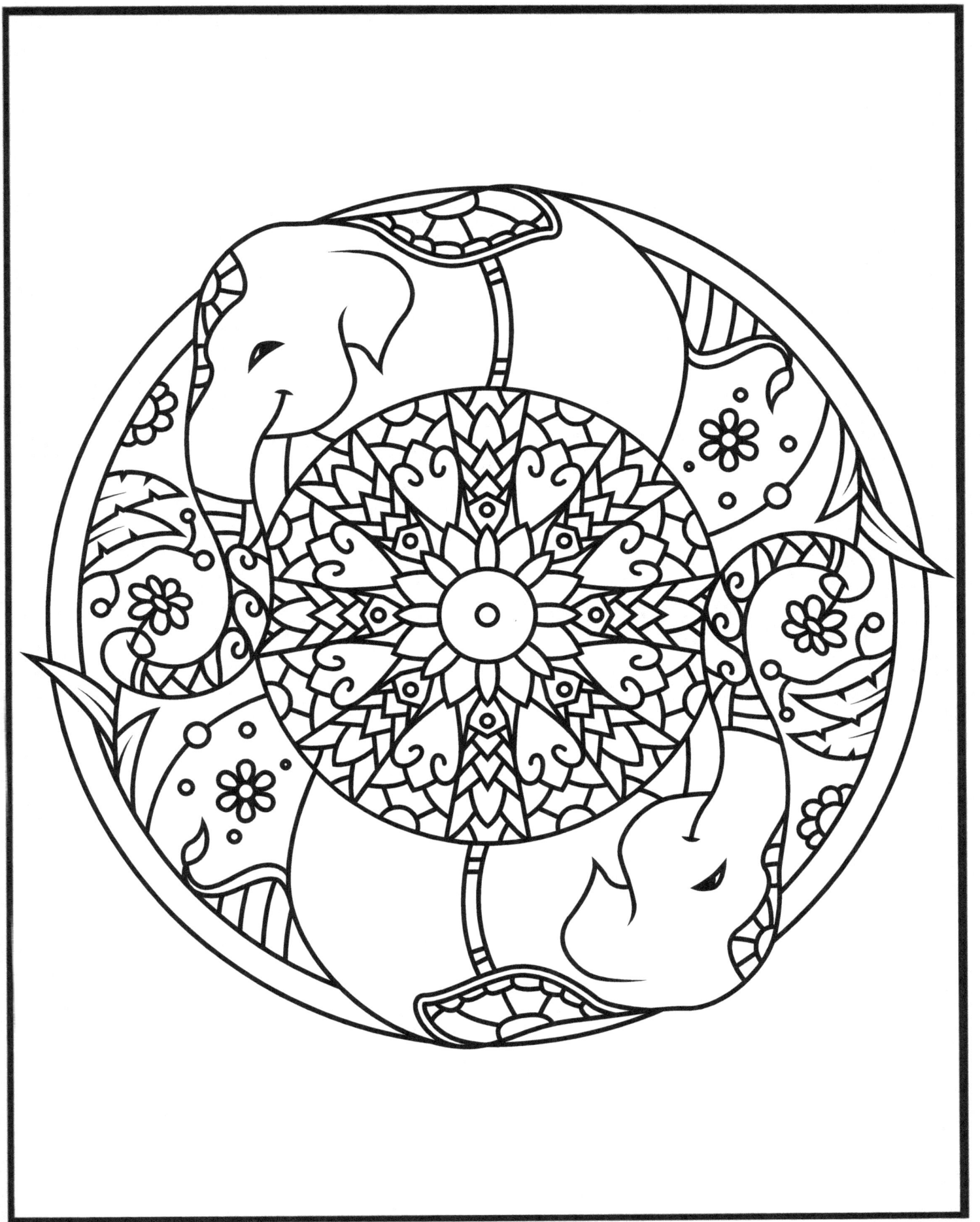

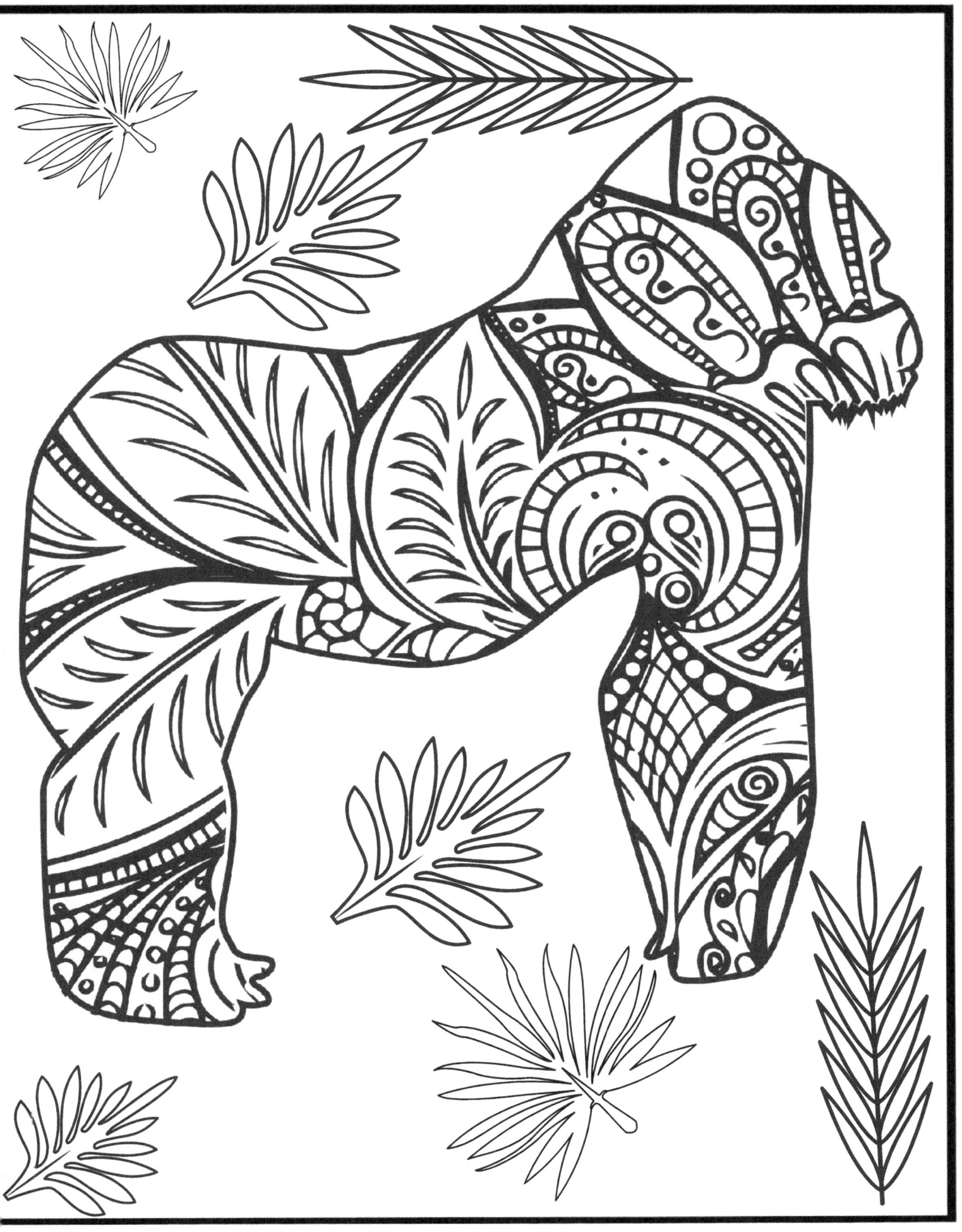

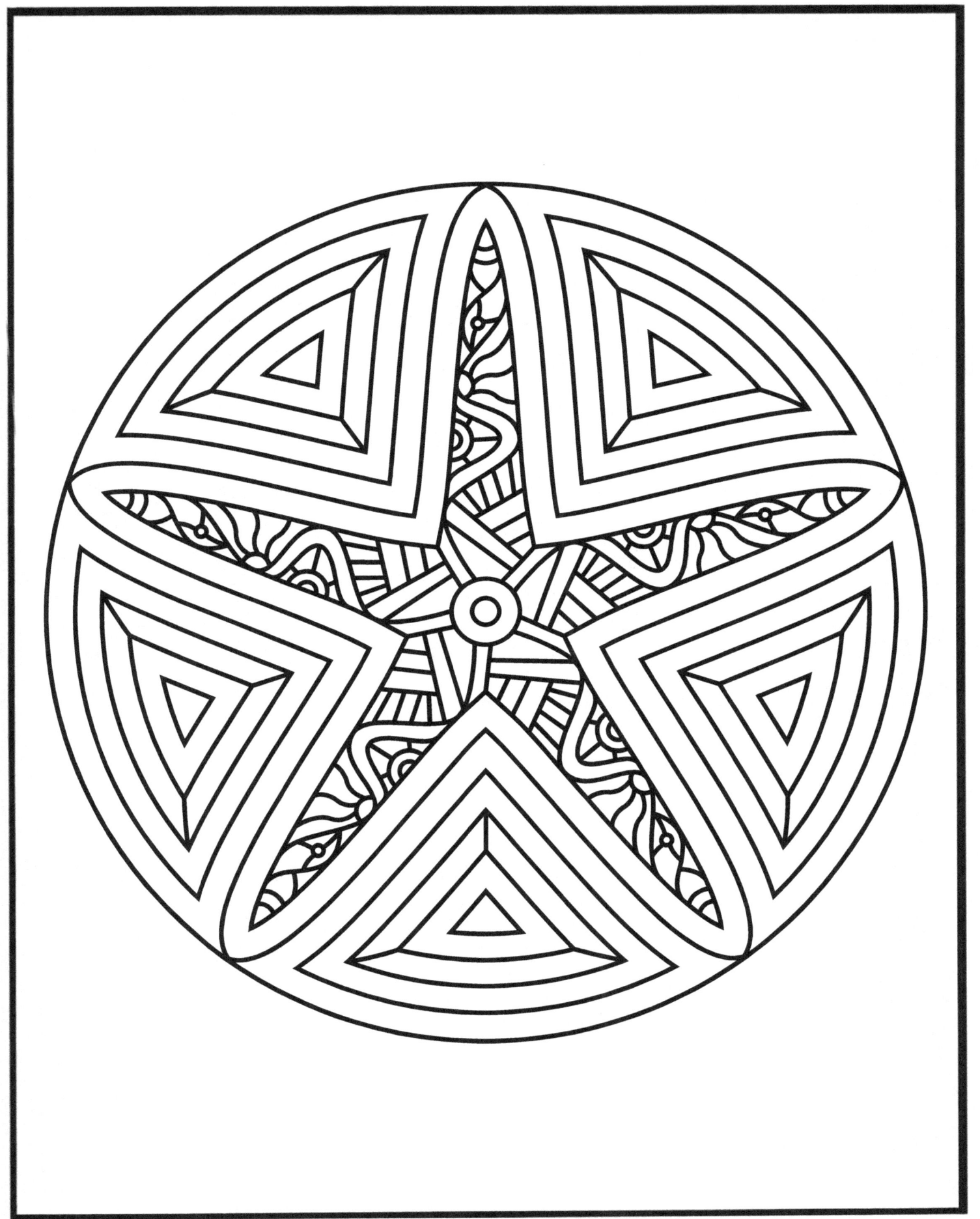

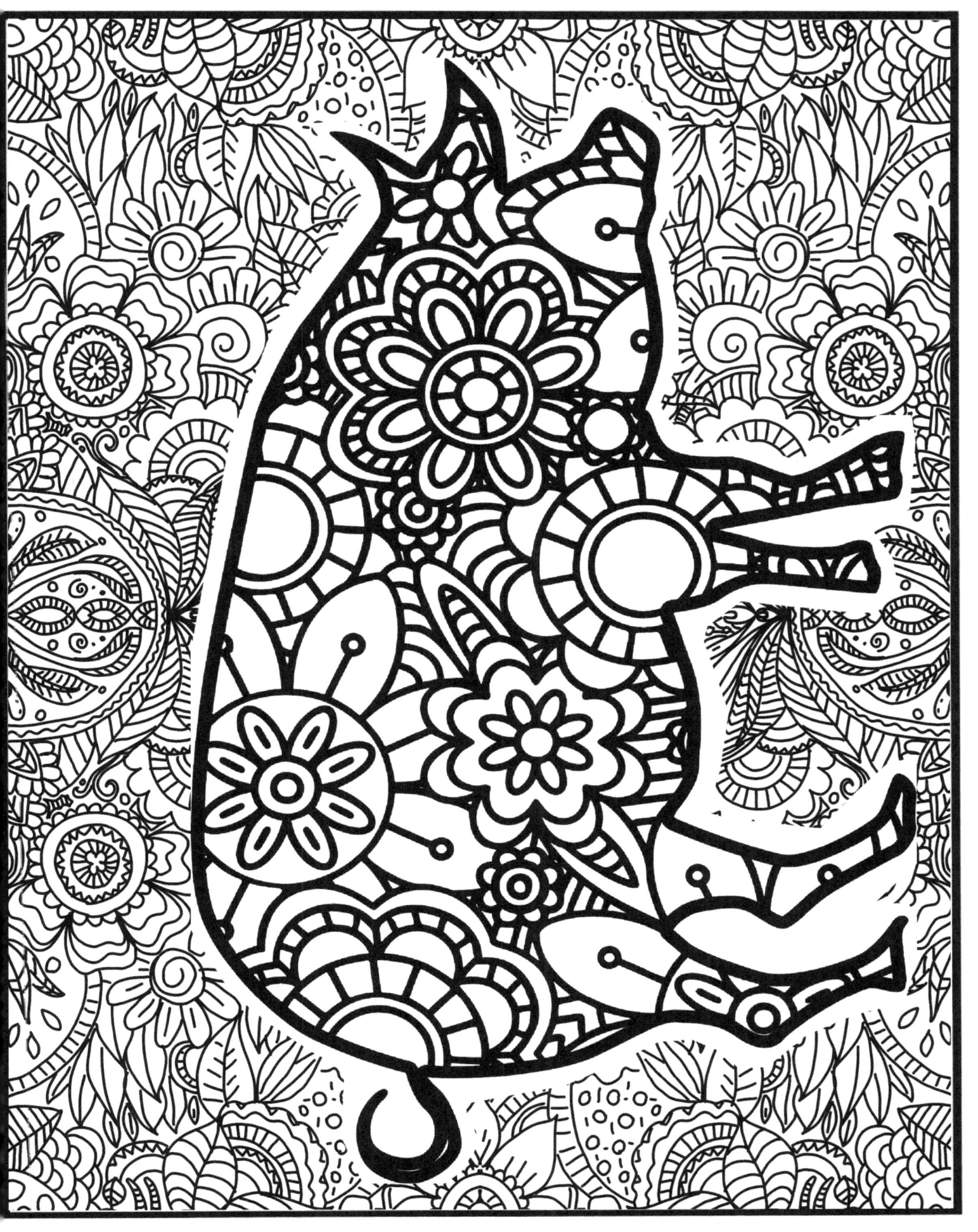

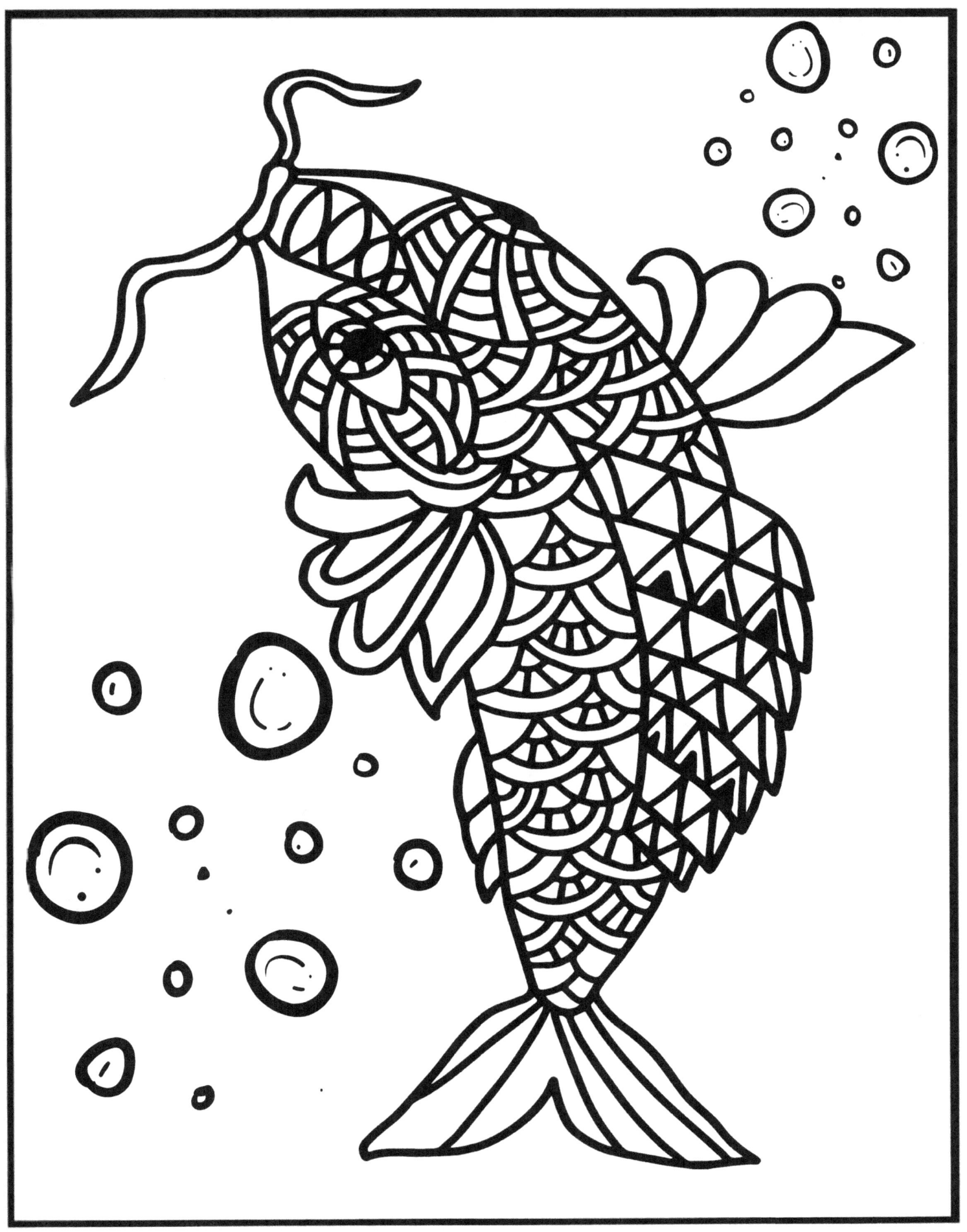

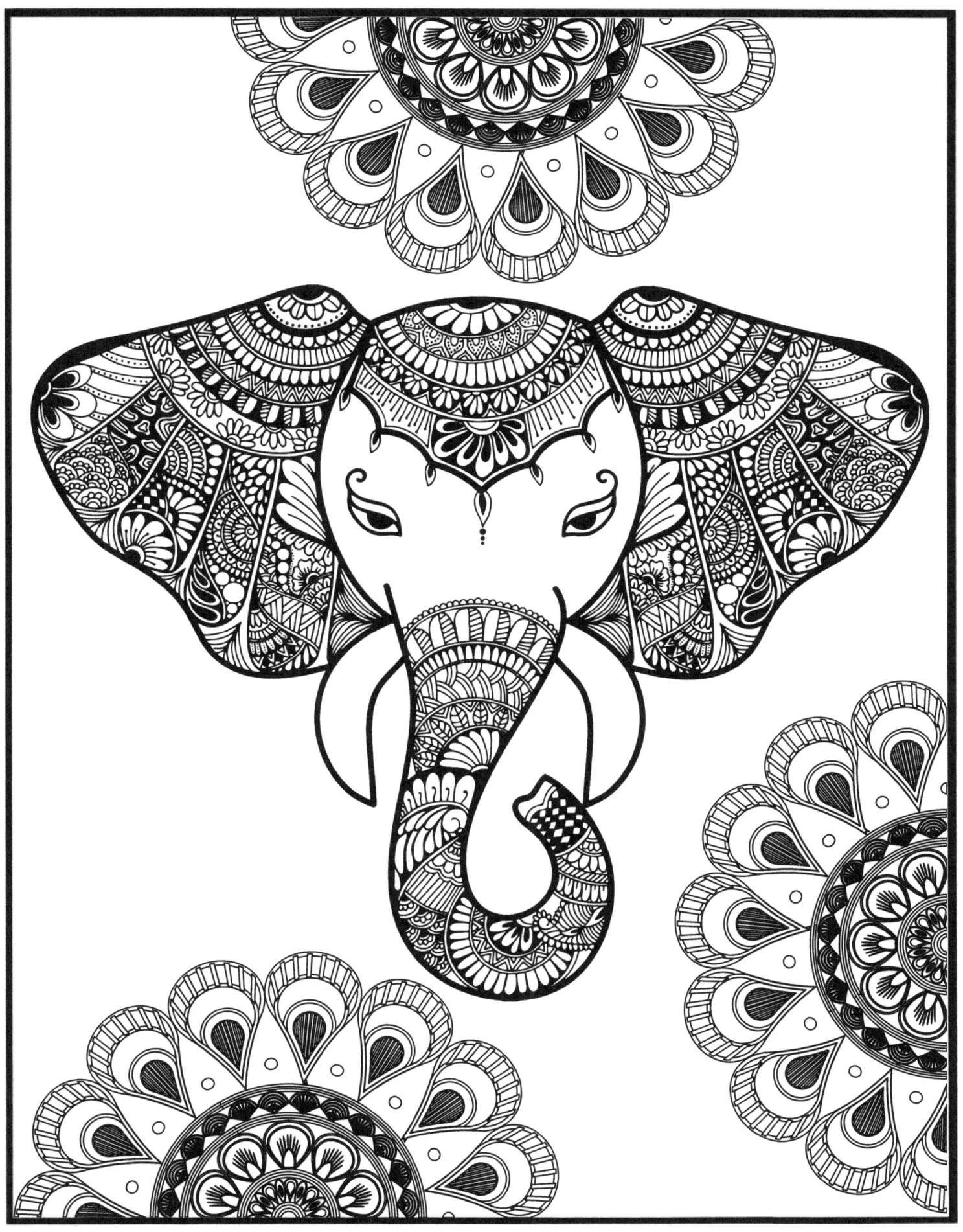

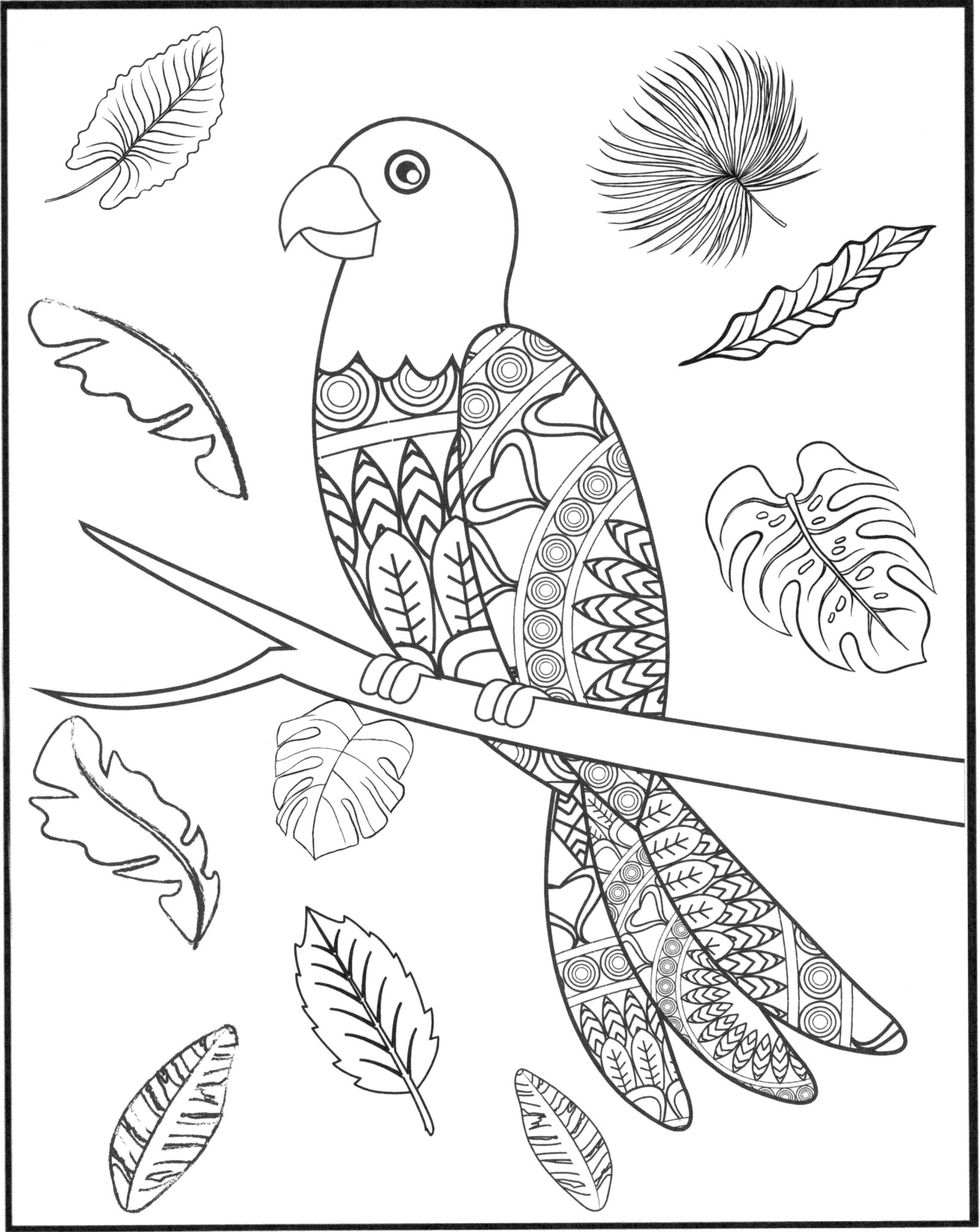

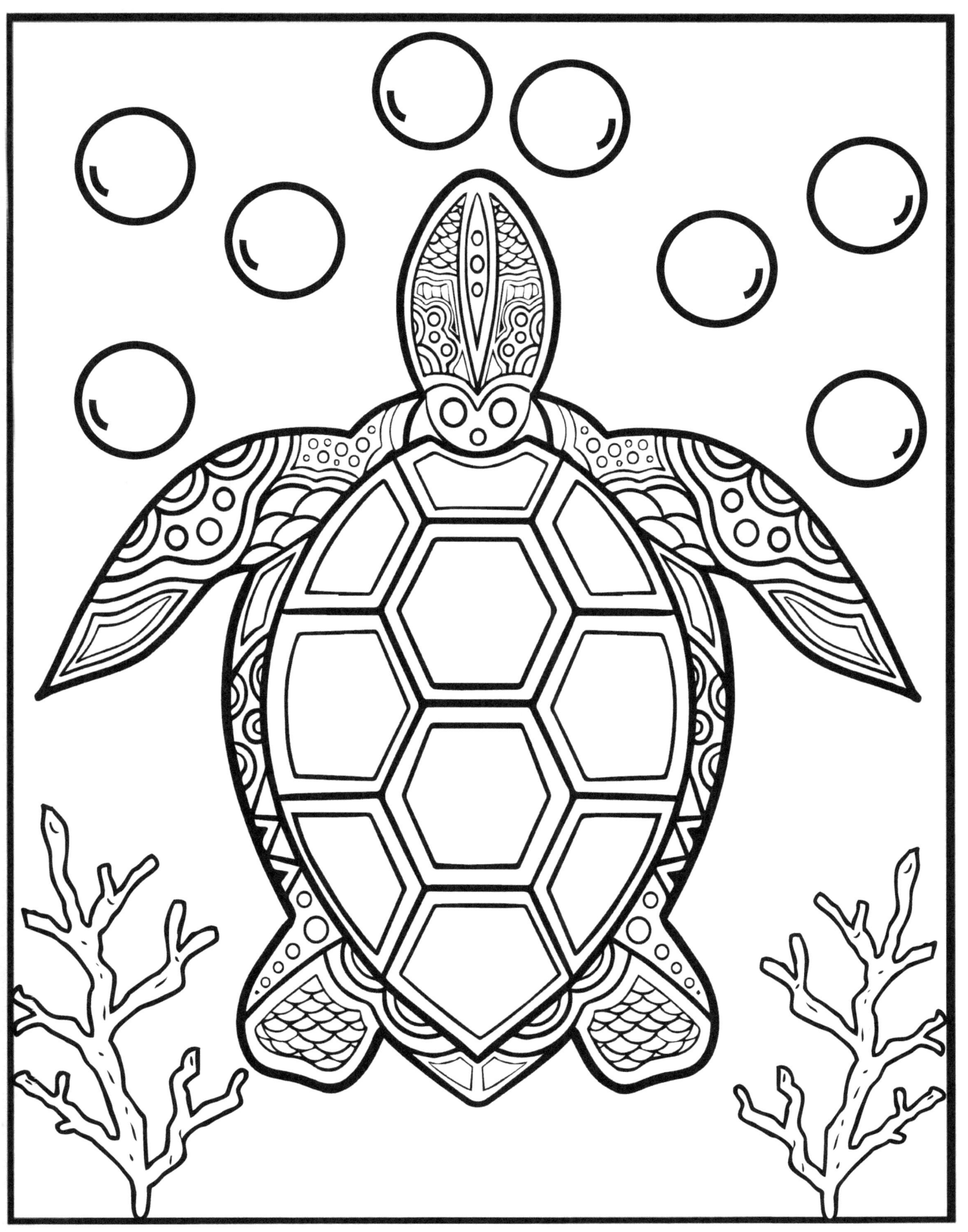

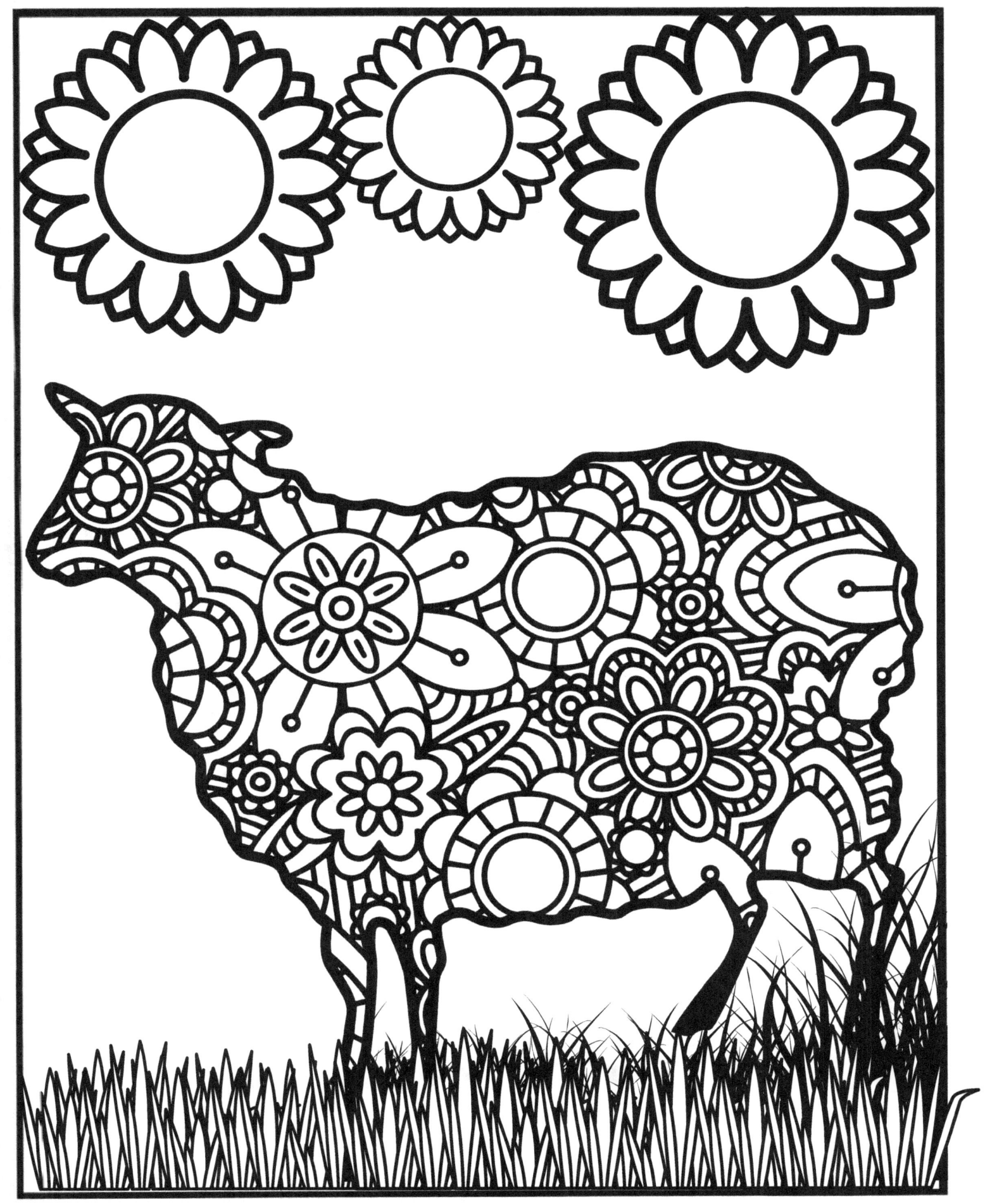

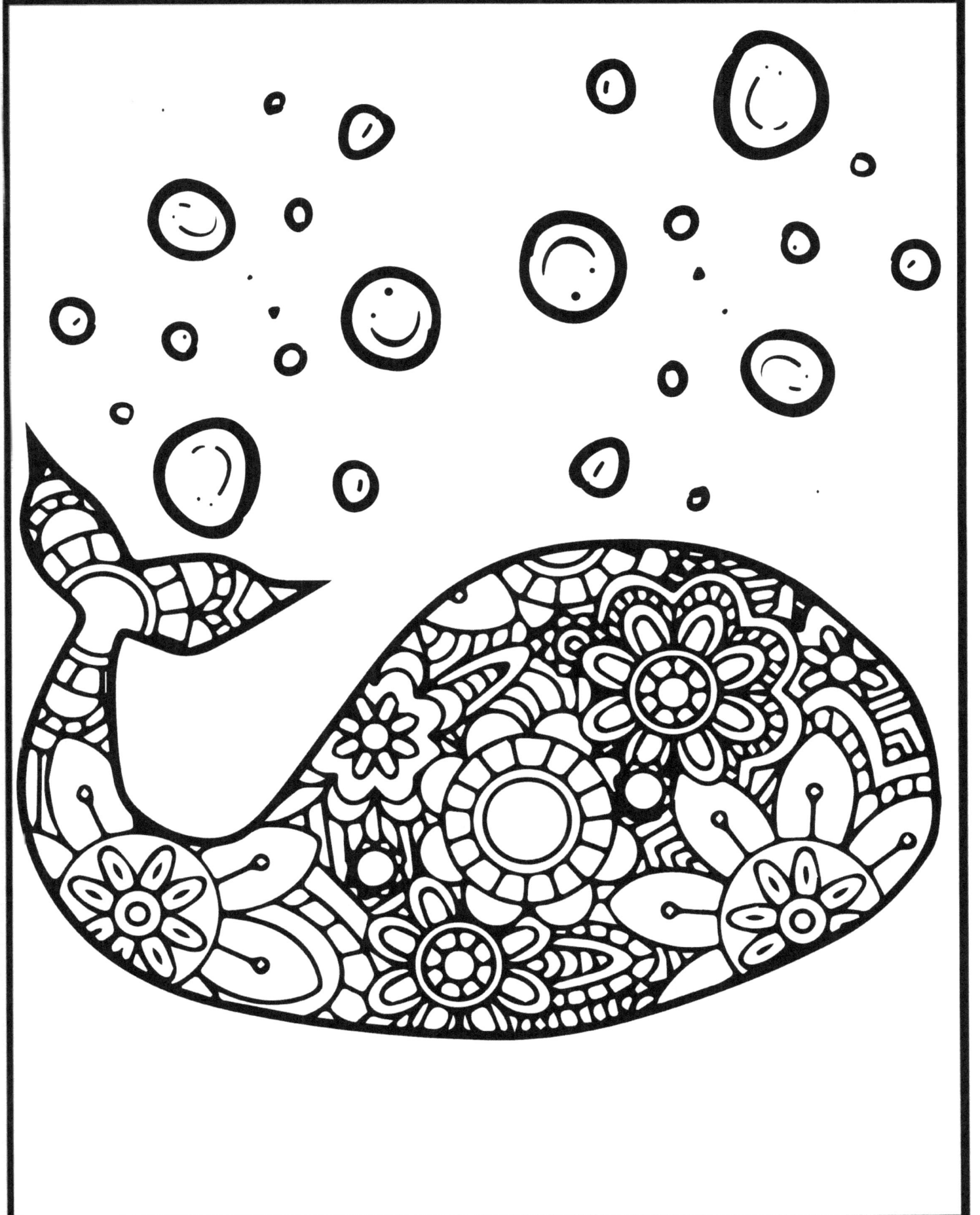

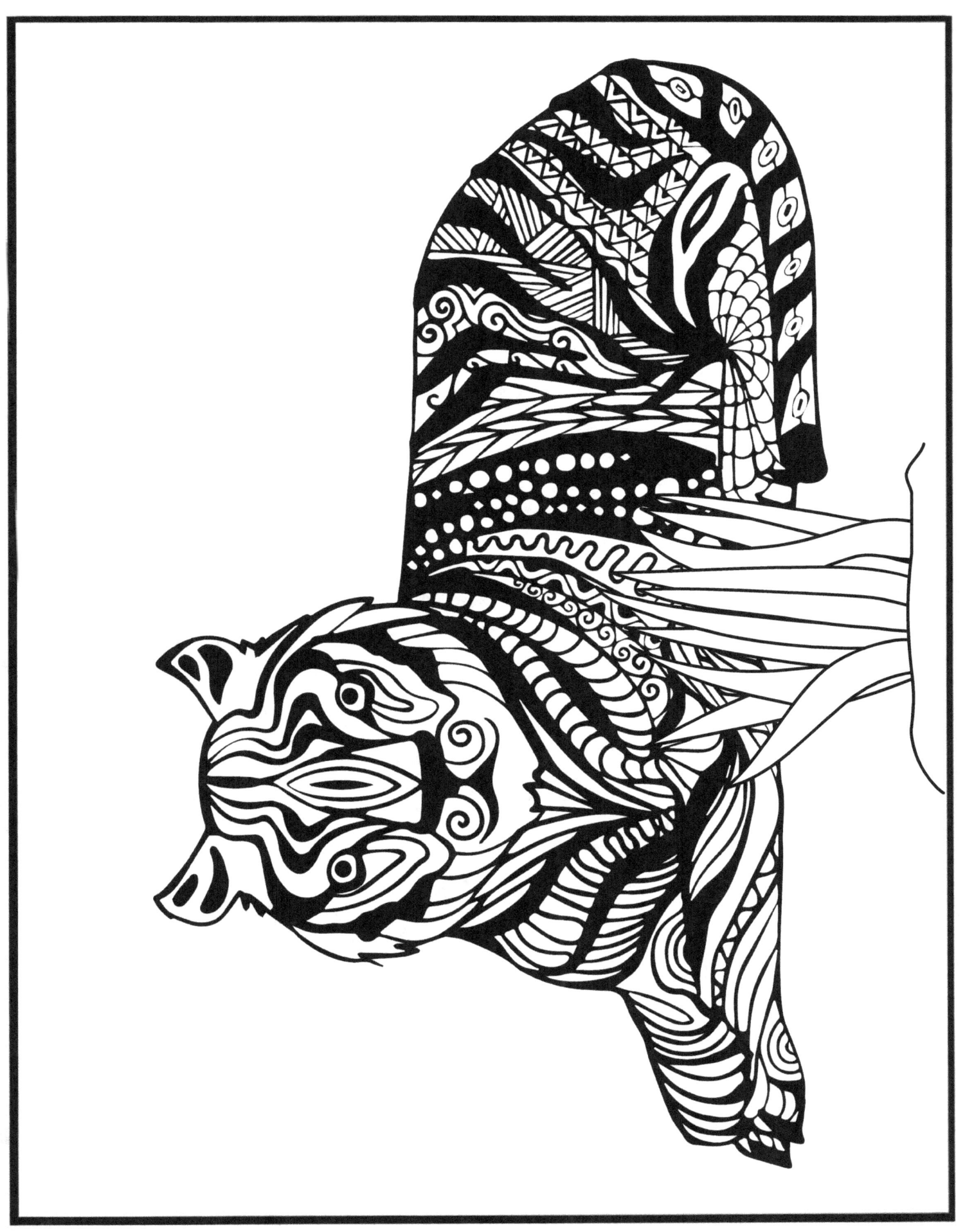

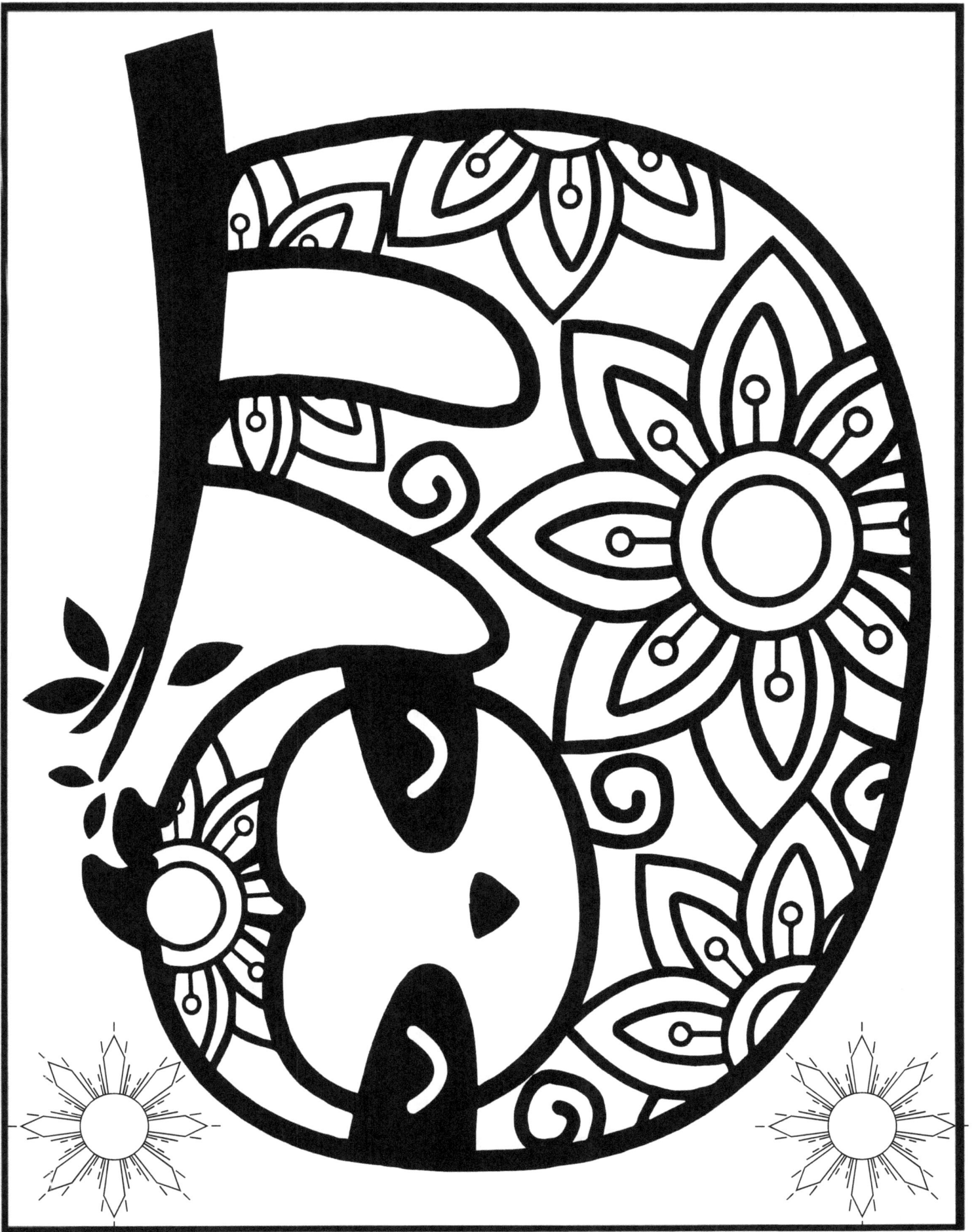

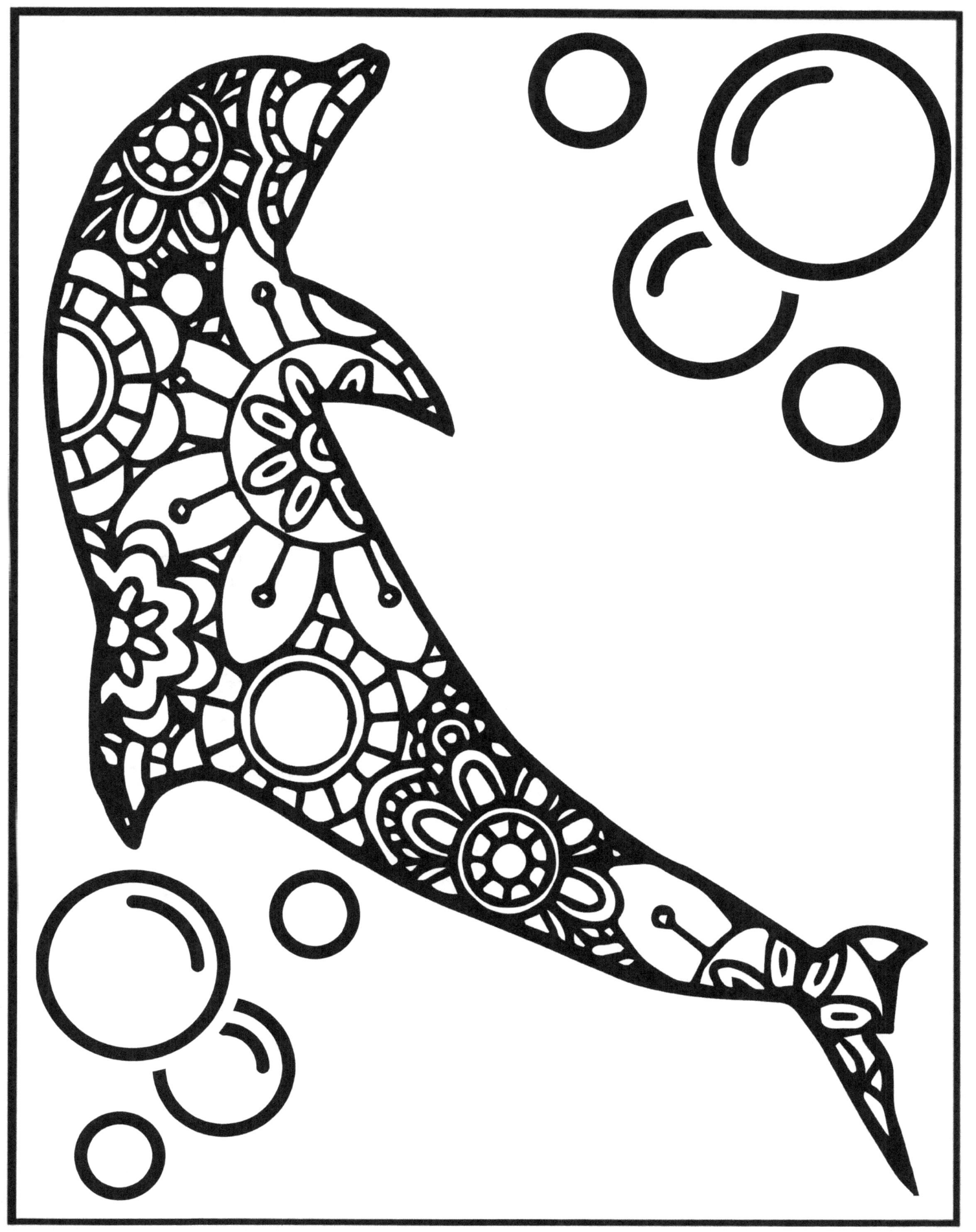

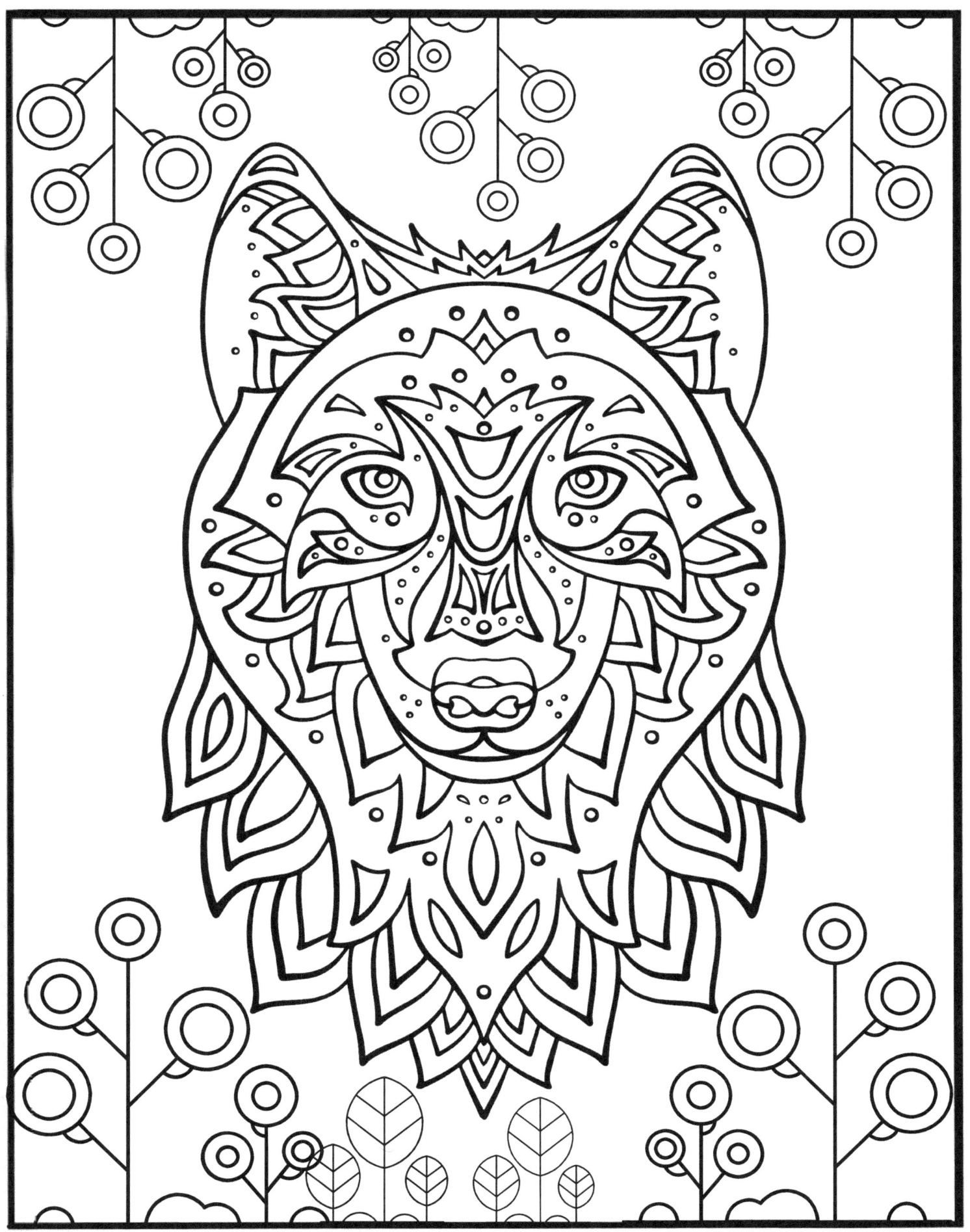

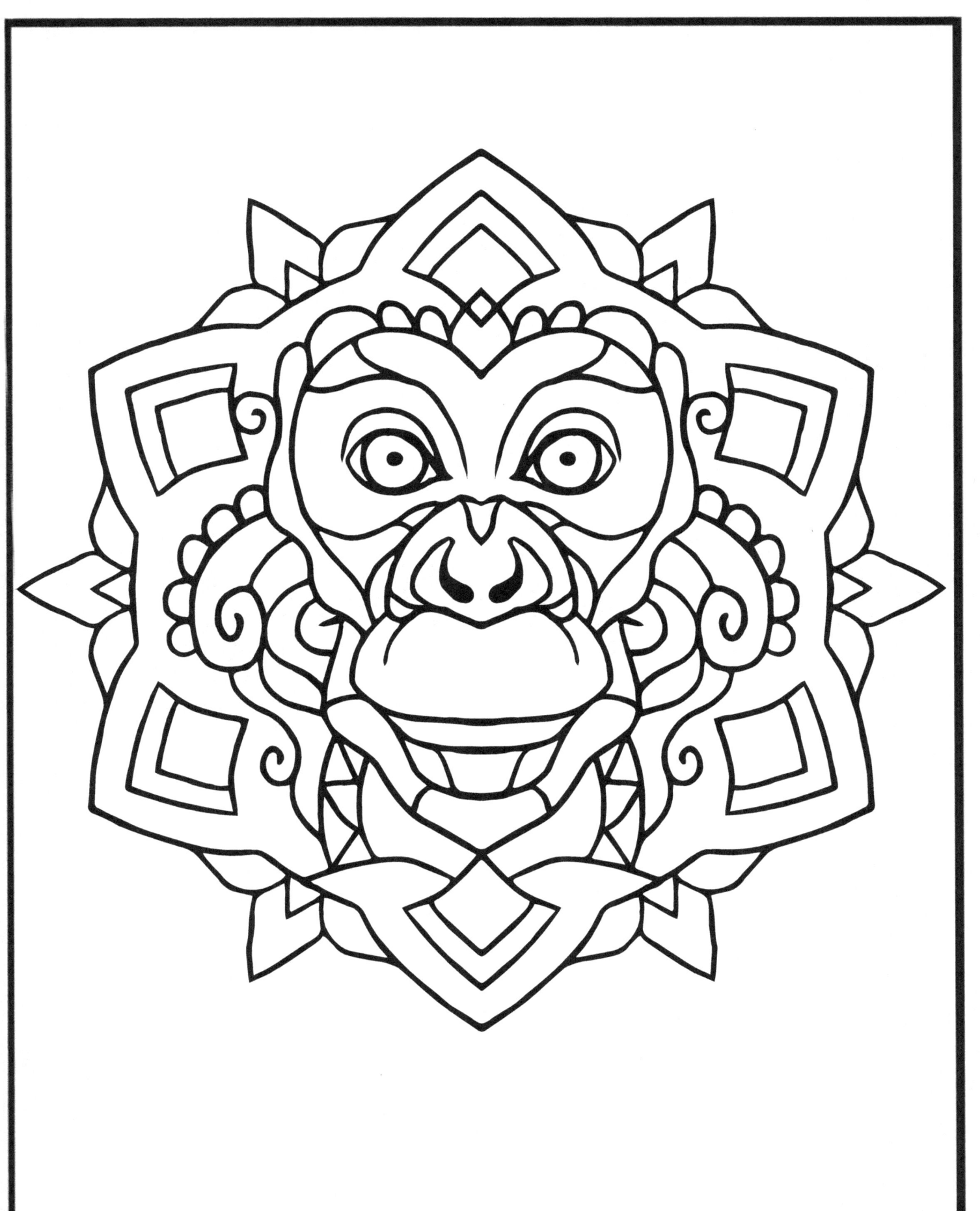

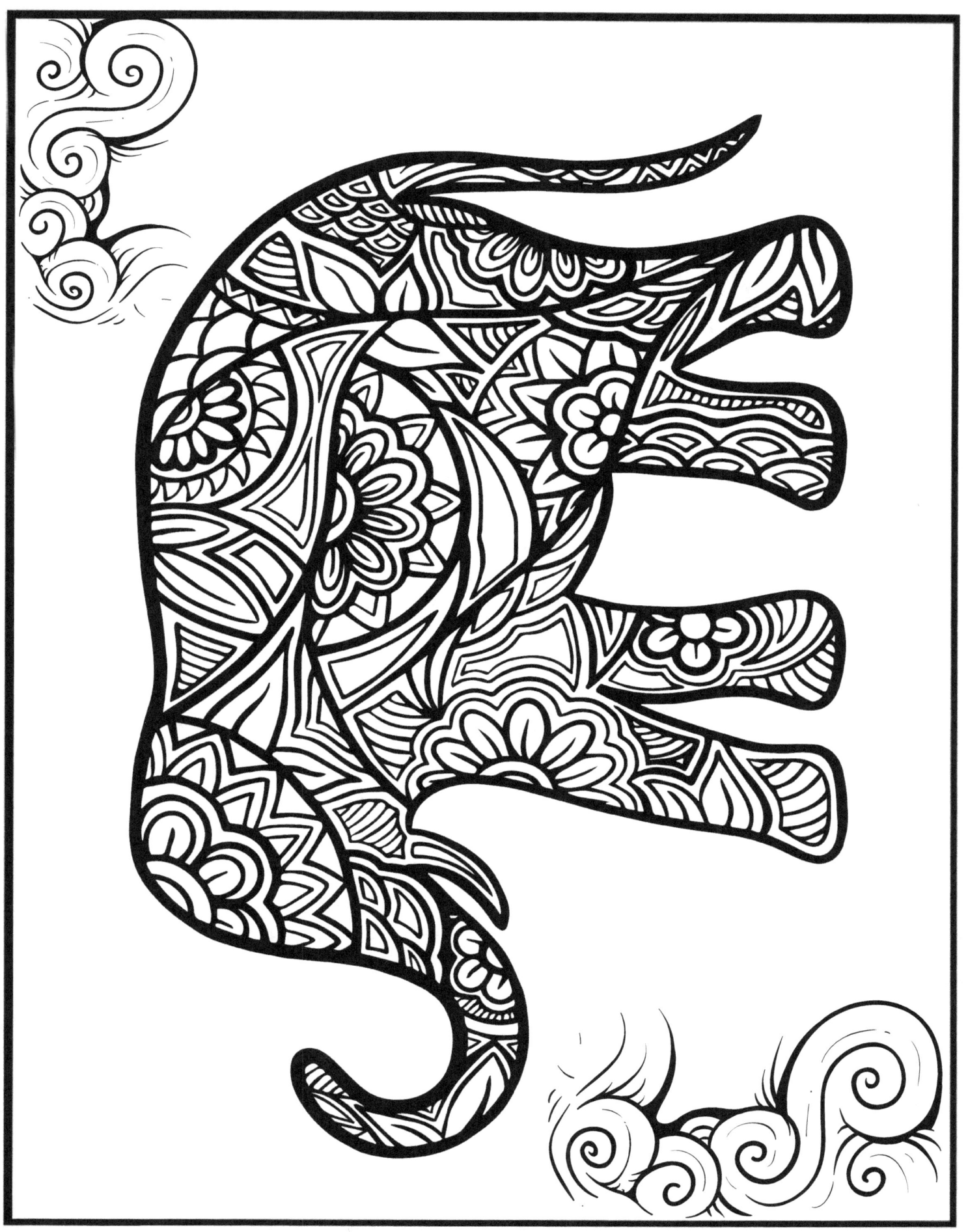

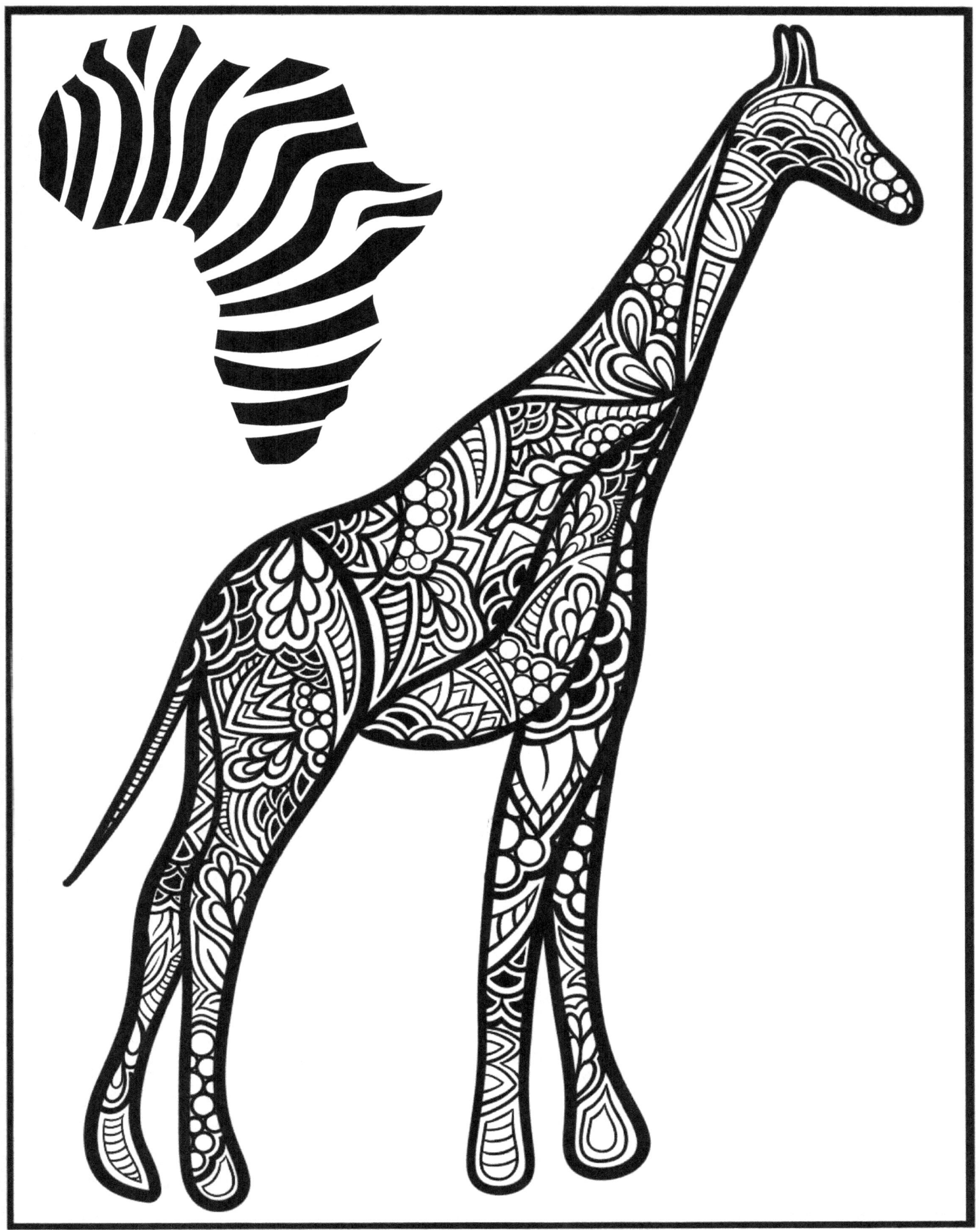

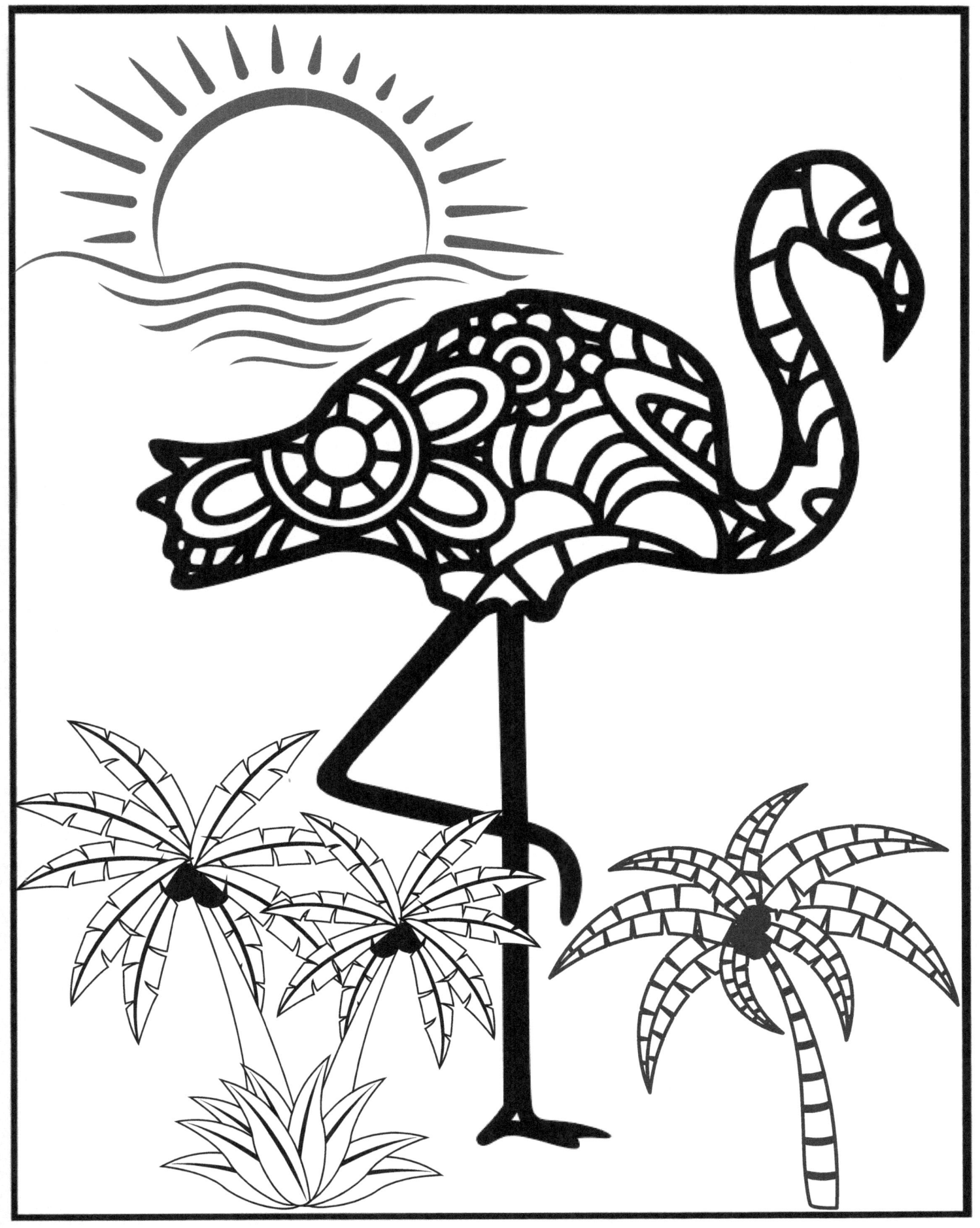

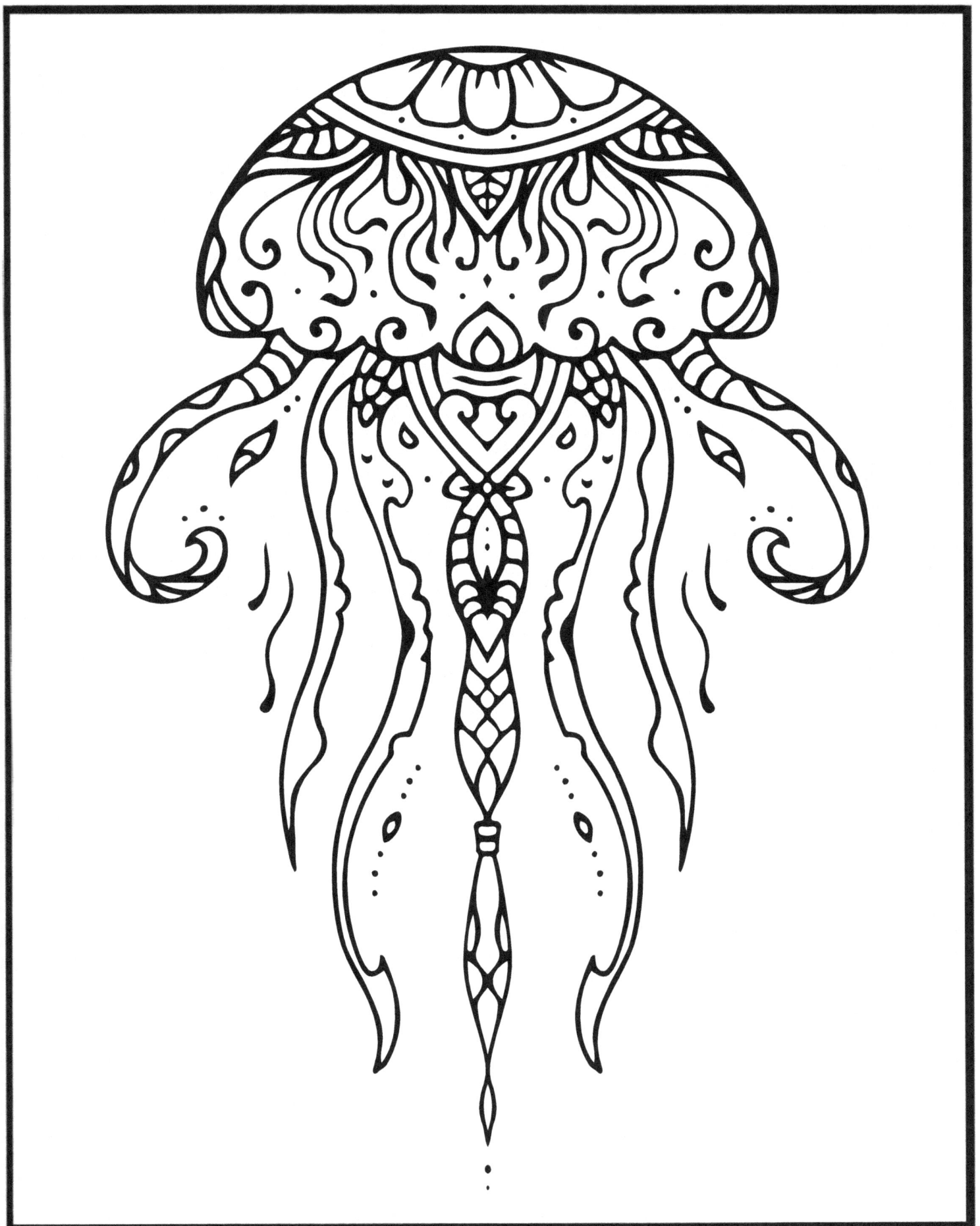

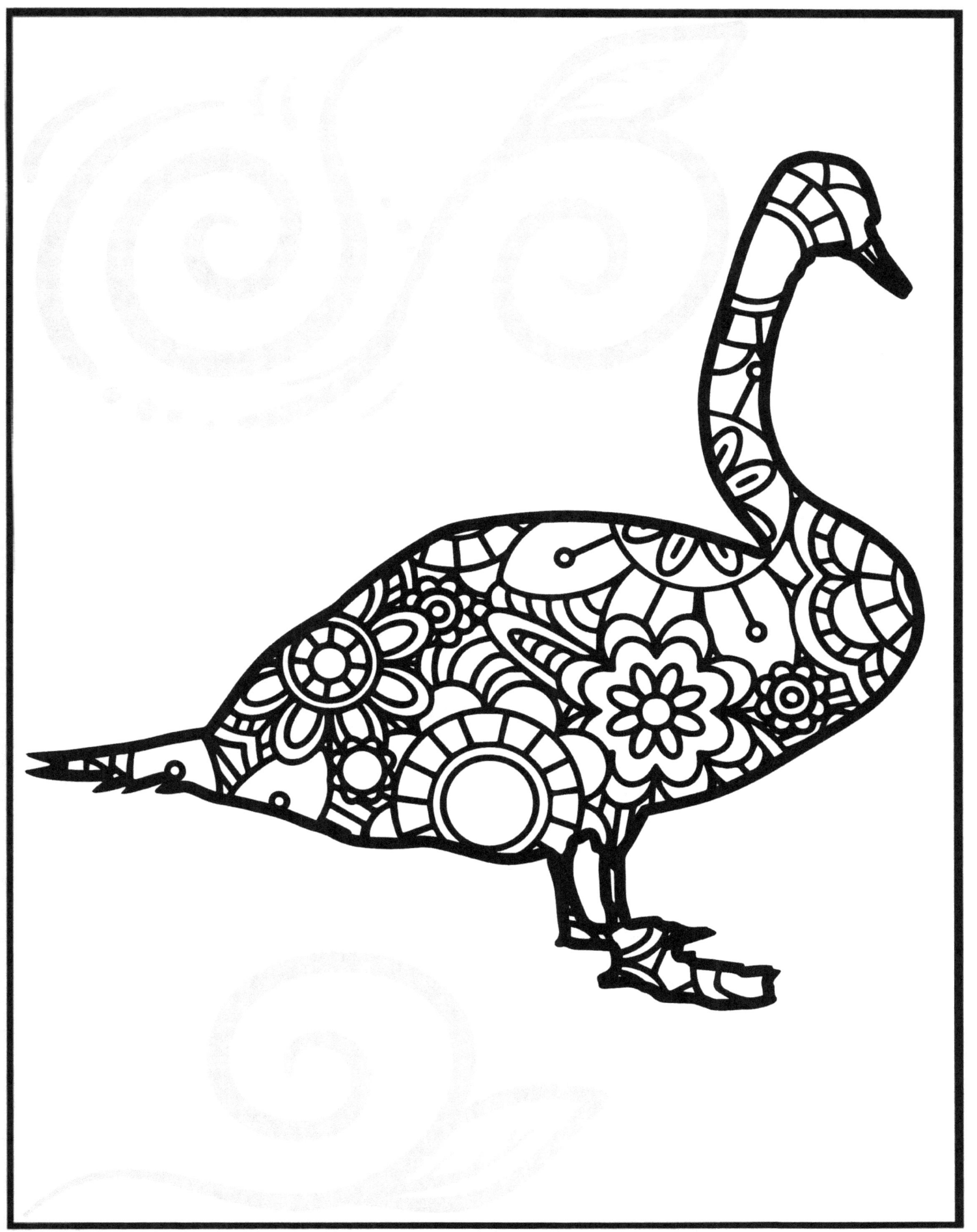

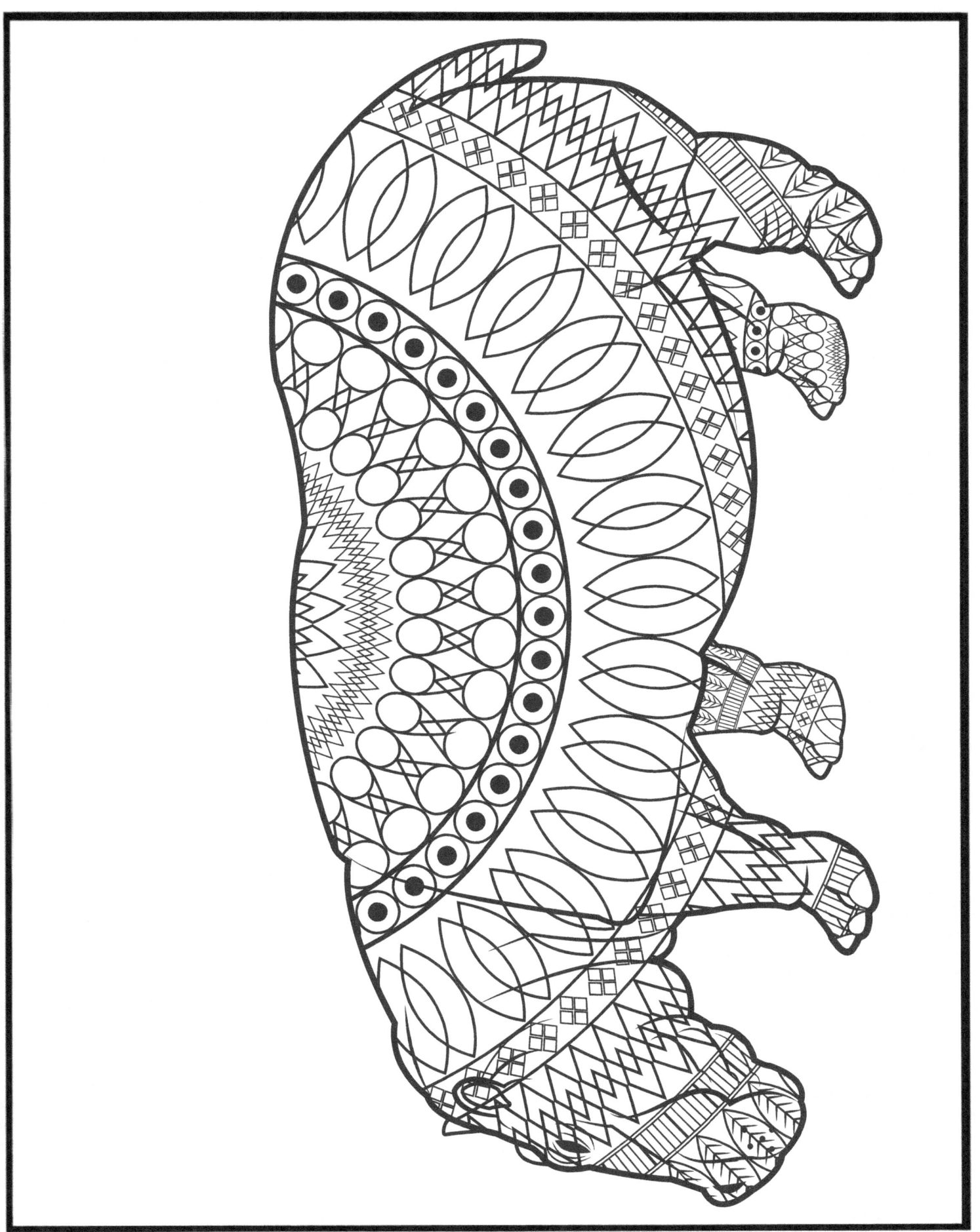

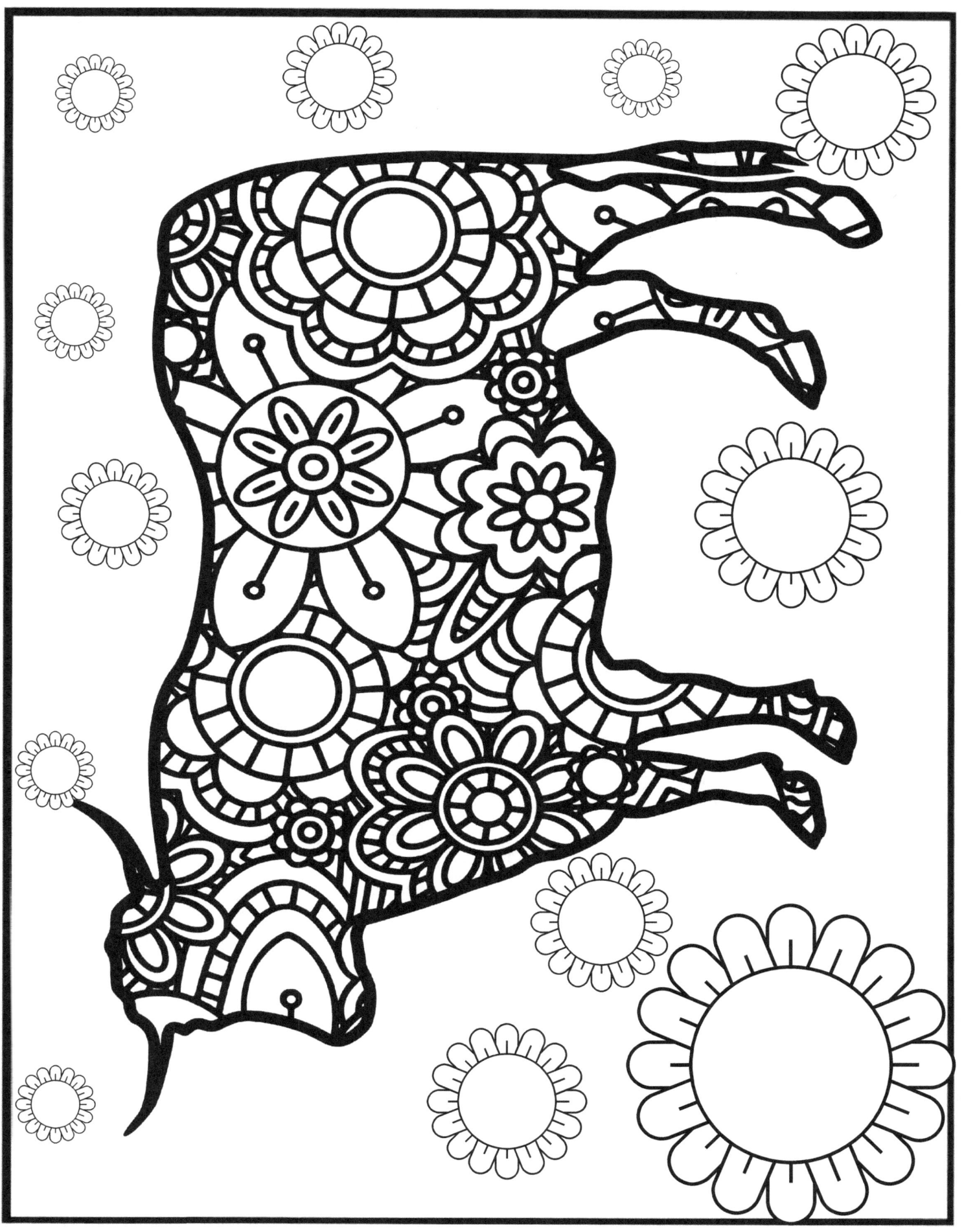

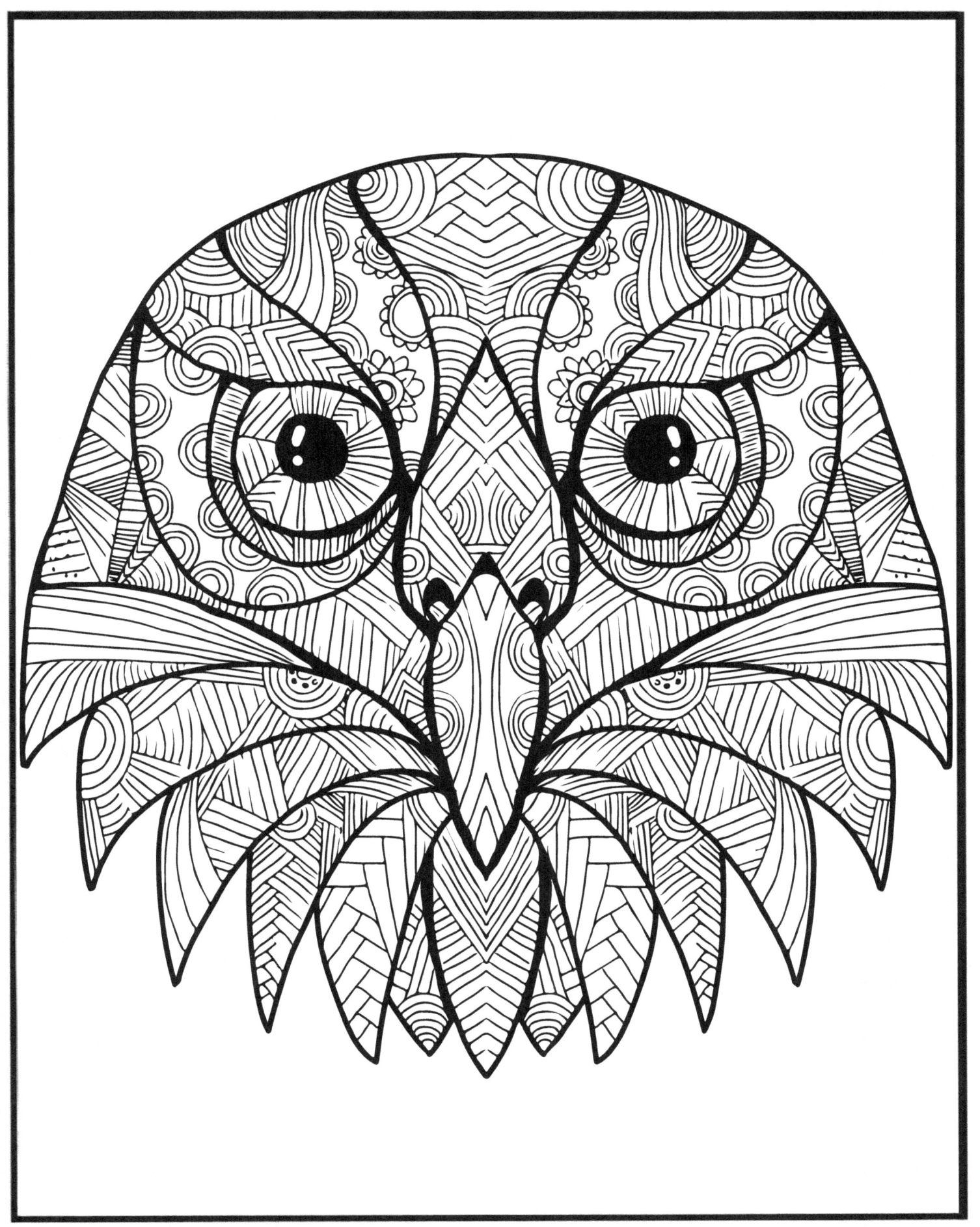

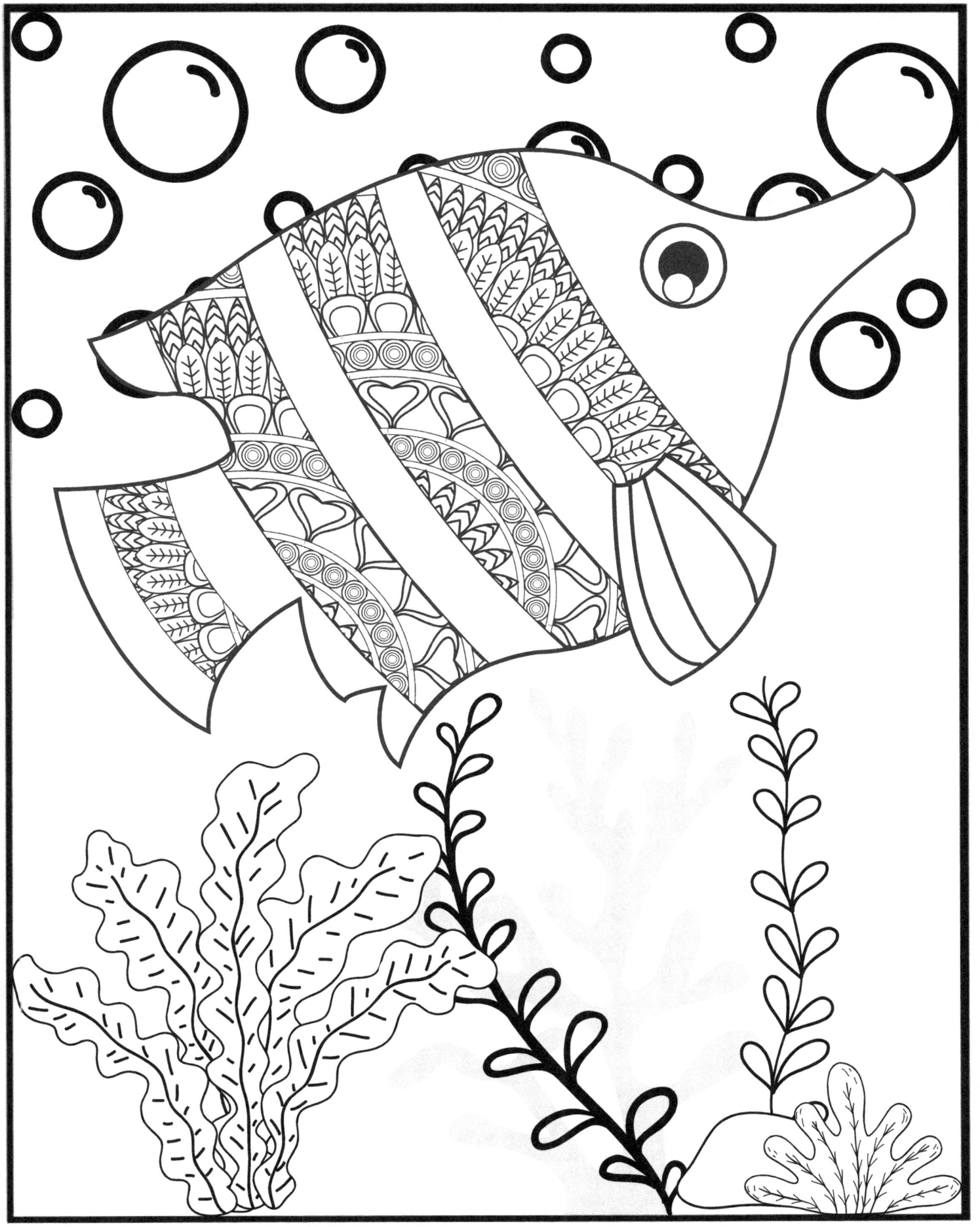

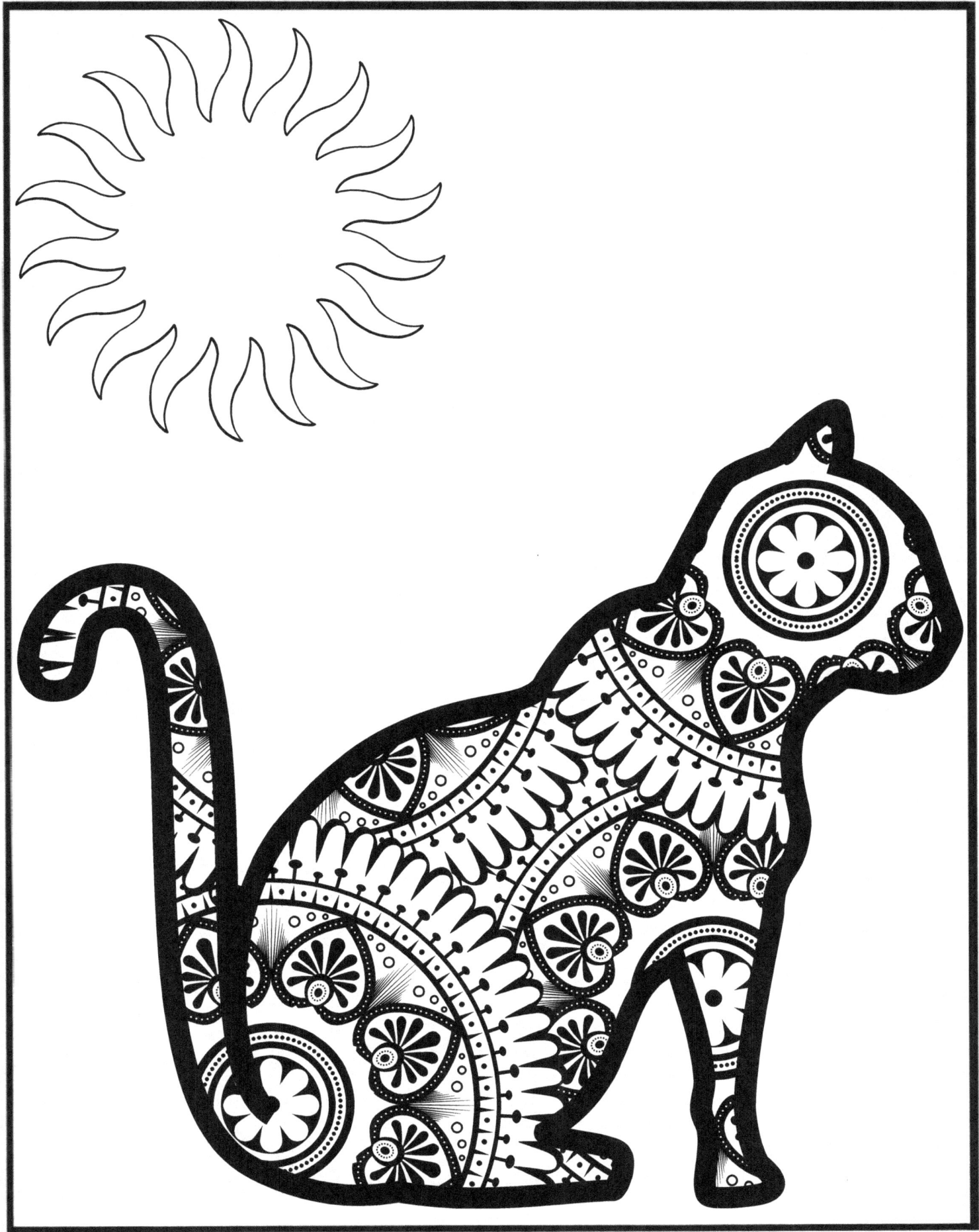

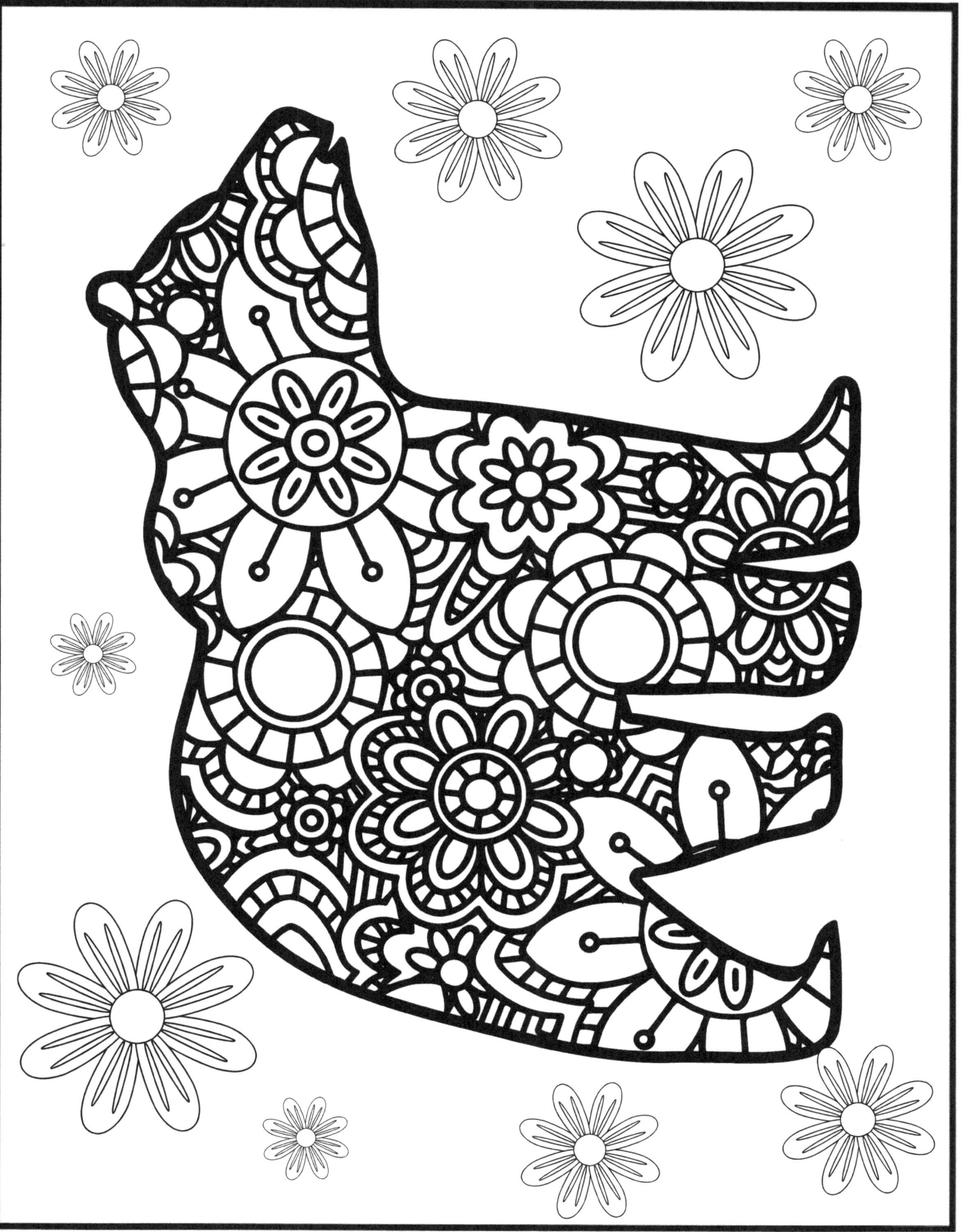

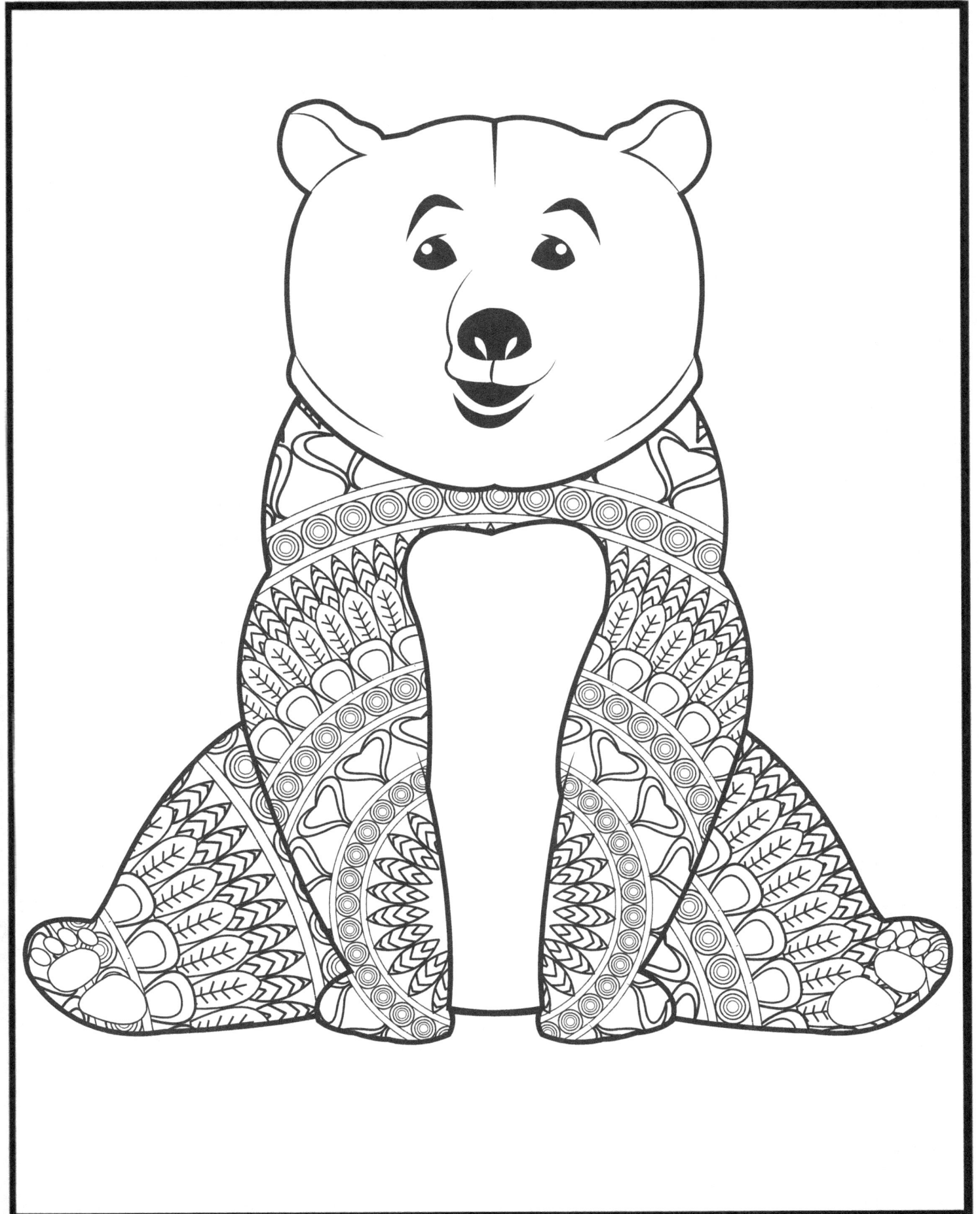

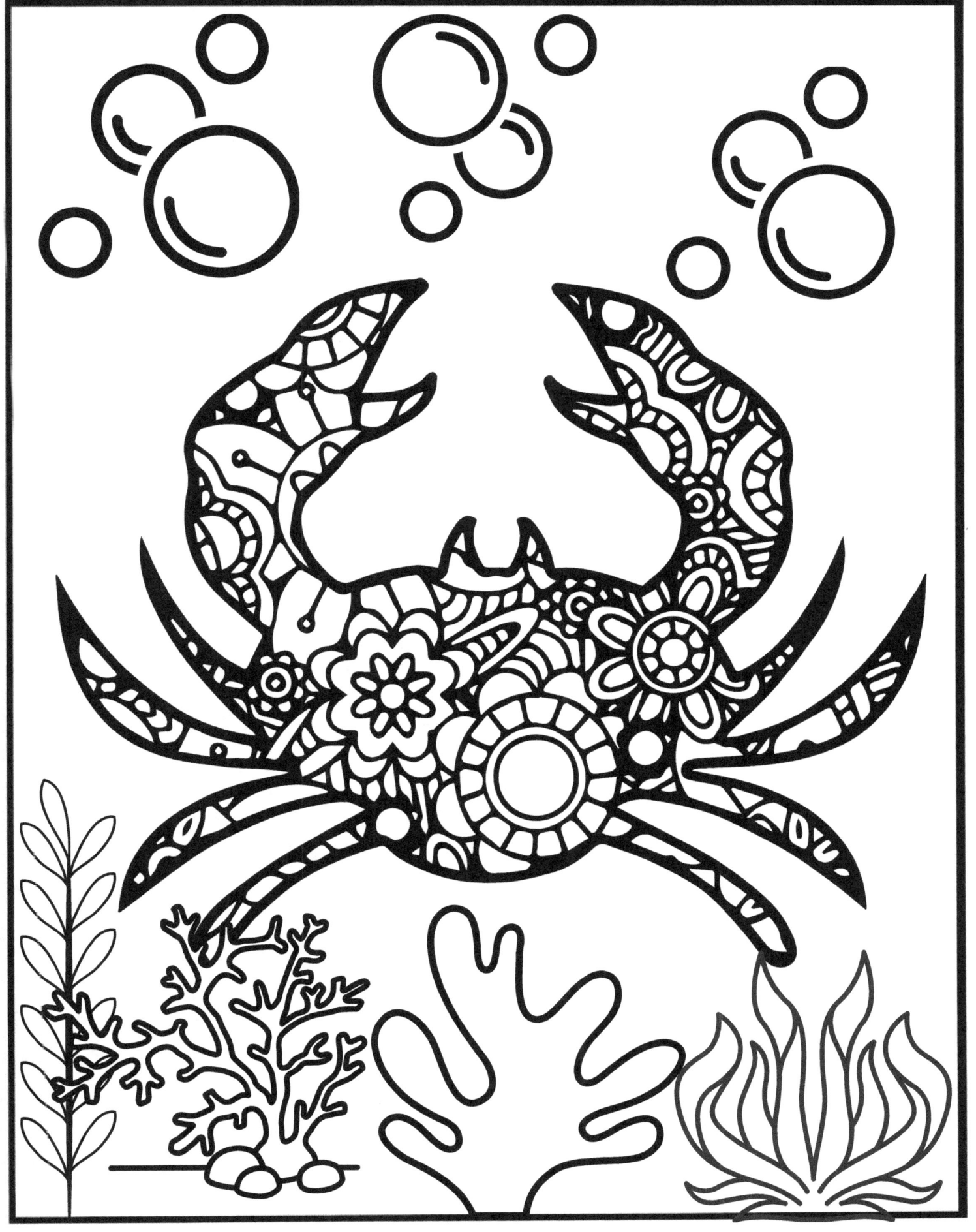

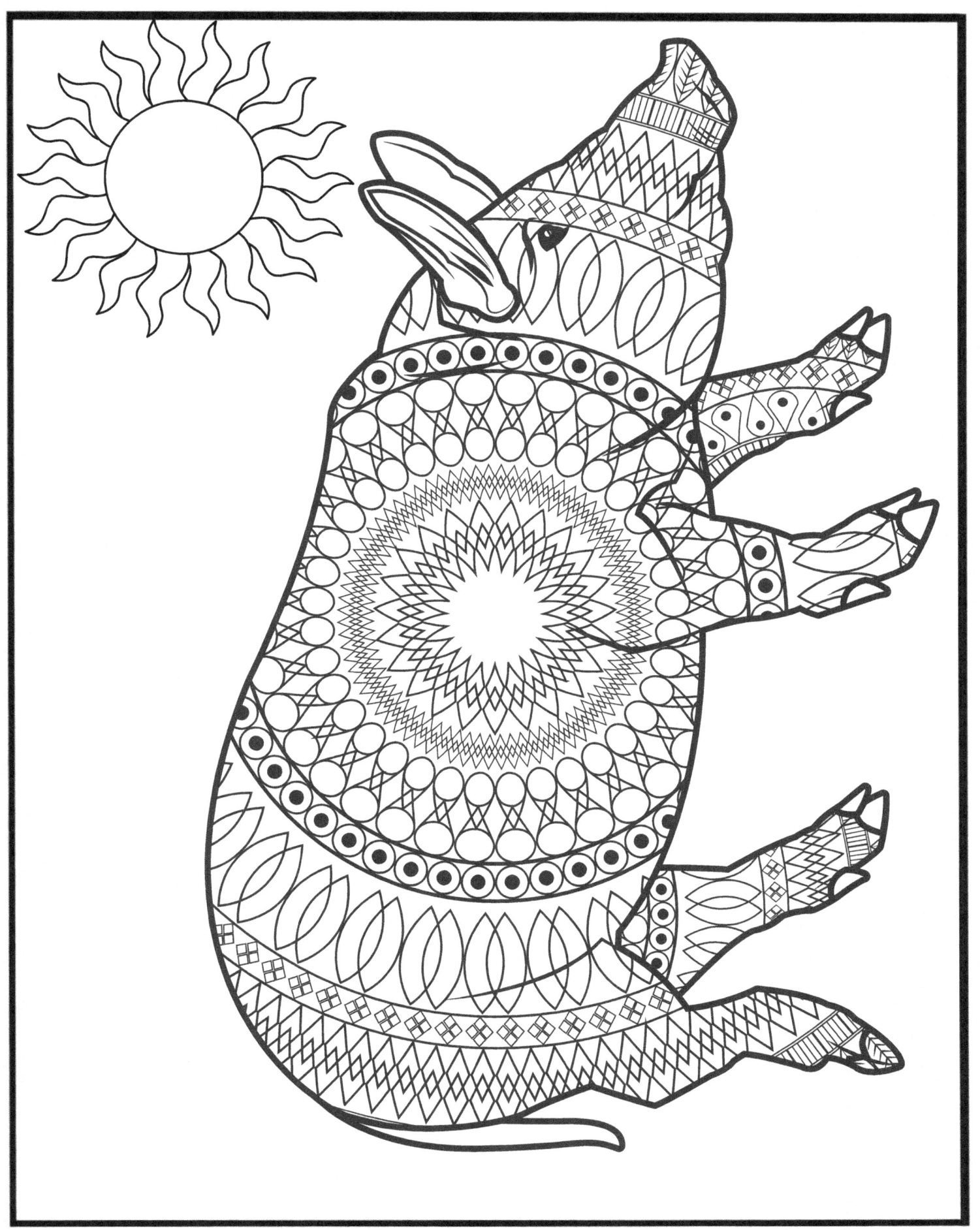

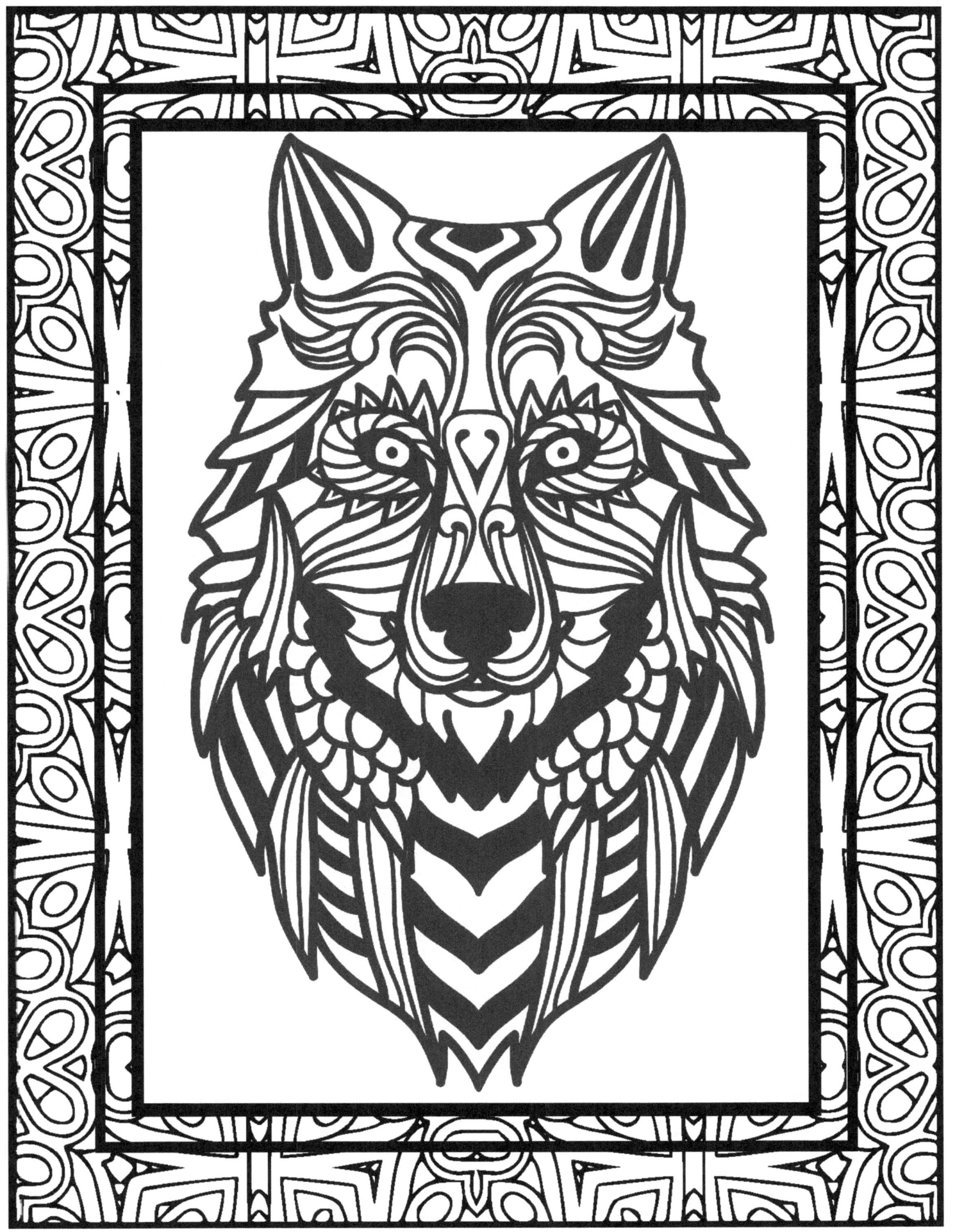

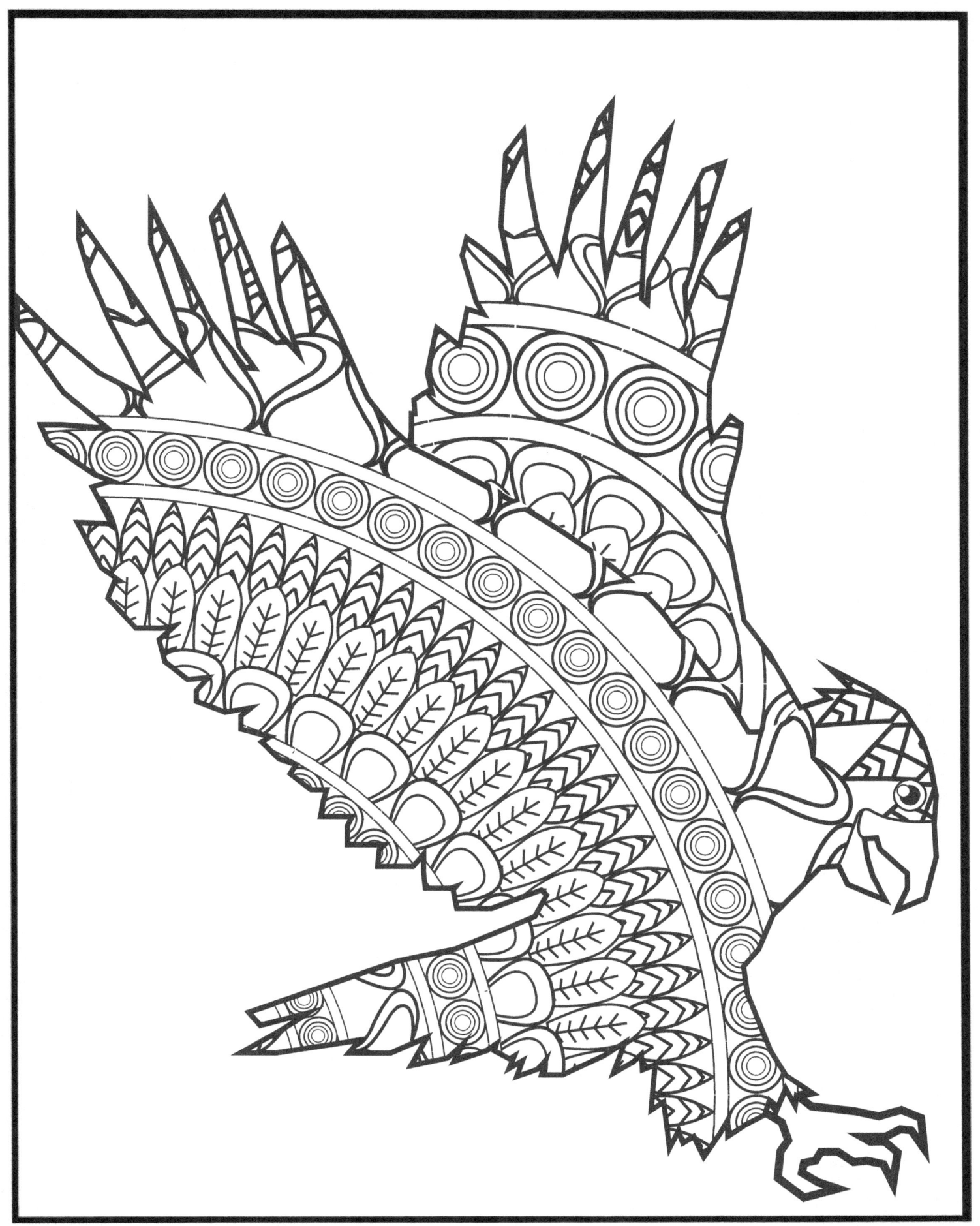

Zen Animals Coloring Book by Puzzler Squad
5233 Bellflower Blvd, Lakewood, CA 90713-1814
www.puzzlersquad.com

Cover by Stephanie Perez.

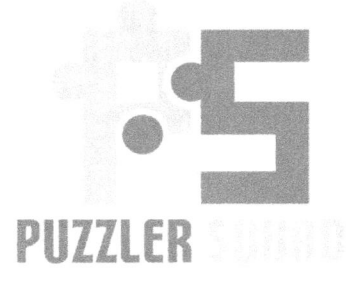

PUZZLER SQUAD

Join Puzzler Squad Today

and receive free printable puzzles every week in your email.

Each week you will receive 7 or more puzzles and activities that have never been published before. We will also let you know when our next puzzle or activity book is released.

You can optin at puzzlersquad.com/freeweeklypuzzles

www.ingramcontent.com/pod-product-compliance
Lightning Source LLC
Chambersburg PA
CBHW081520220526
45467CB00010B/2987